CISTERCIANS
AND CLUNIACS

ST BERNARD'S *APOLOGIA* TO ABBOT WILLIAM

Translated by MICHAEL CASEY ocso

Introduction by JEAN LECLERCQ osb

†

CISTERCIAN PUBLICATIONS

This translation first appeared in *Bernard of Clairvaux: Treatises I,* The Works of Bernard of Clairvaux, 1. The Cistercian Fathers Series, Volume One (Spencer, Massachusetts–Shannon, Ireland, 1970). It is based on the critical Latin edition prepared by Jean Leclercq and Henri Rochais under the sponsorship of the Order of Cistercians and published by Editiones Cistercienses, Piazza Tempio di Diana 14, 1-00153 Rome.

cistercian publications

*The work of Cistercian Publications is made possible in part
by support from Western Michigan University to
The Institute of Cistercian Studies.*

CUSTOMER SERVICE:

The United States: Liturgical Press
Saint John's Abbey Collegeville, MN 56321-7500
sales@litpress.org

ISBN 0 87907 102 8

Printed in the United States of America

INTRODUCTION

THE APOLOGIA was written in 1125, when St Bernard was thirty-five years old. He had been a Cistercian monk for twelve years, and abbot of Clairvaux for ten. We know that by this time both his literary talents and his spiritual outlook were fully developed. He had already written some of his letters, as well as the first redaction of his homilies *In Praise of the Virgin Mary*[1] and about the same time he was also engaged in the composition of *The Steps of Humility*.[2] Neither of these two treatises was polemic in character, so that the *Apologia* was a step in a new direction.

This tract was a product of the controversy which arose between the Cistercians and the adherents of an established monasticism, regarding the interpretation of the Rule of St Benedict. In the older monasteries—the ones we today would call "Benedictine," and whose members were known in those days from the color of their habits as "Black Monks"—a long process of development had brought about a situation in which the life of the monks was moderated, not only by the Rule, but also by a set of customs based on the ecclesiastical, liturgical, economic, sociological and psychological conditions of a former age. In contrast stood the Cistercians. Like all the new orders that made their appearance about this time, they wished to live more simply and poorly, and their habit of

1. Cf. *S. Bernardi Opera* (Rome: Editiones Cistercienses, 1966), IV, p. 3.
2. *Ibid.*, III (1963), pp. 3f.

plain undyed wool was a symbol of this aspiration. The "Grey Monks," as they were called, wanted to live according to the Rule of St Benedict, to return to the basic pattern of Benedictine life which had, they thought, been obscured and obstructed by the customs that had accumulated over the years. The founders of such orders had no desire to reform the existing system of monasticism, as if to suggest that it was completely degenerate. Their aim was to establish a new form of monastic life, one that would be closer to the Rule, and at the same time, more in harmony with the contemporary situation.[3]

The reaction of the Black Monks was instinctive; they felt slighted and lost no time in defending themselves. Meanwhile, some of the Cistercians, rightly proud of their Order, were becoming self-satisfied and critical of the Black Monks. Of course not all monks were involved, but the difference of opinion was sufficiently stimulating to provoke, within the space of a hundred years or so, no less than eleven tracts, which trace out for us the development of monastic thought during this period.[4] Of these the most famous is St Bernard's *Apologia*.

Origin of the Apologia

We are fortunate in having fairly detailed knowledge of the circumstances surrounding the composition of the *Apologia*. It may be worthwhile to recall them briefly, since this gives us an opportunity of seeing St Bernard at work, slowly bringing a book to completion. In the present case the process lasted at least six months.

3. I have tried to show this in my article "The Intention of the Founders of the Cistercian Order" in *The Cistercian Spirit: A Symposium* (Cistercian Studies Series, 3).

4. A list of these tracts will be found in the bibliography. They are analyzed by A. Wilmart in "Une riposte de l'ancien monachisme au manifeste de S. Bernard" in *Revue bénédictine*, 46 (1934), pp. 296–305. Some of the sociological aspects of the controversy are treated by A. H. Bredero in "The Controversy between Peter the Venerable and Saint Bernard of Clairvaux" in *Petrus Venerabilis, 1156–1956*, pp. 53–71.

Lent in 1125 extended from February 11 to March 28. In the course of it Bernard wrote to Oger, a Canon Regular of Mont-Saint-Eloi in the diocese of Arras. He referred to his booklet *The Steps of Humility*, and to his homilies *In Praise of the Virgin Mary*.[5] About the same time, during the spring, he wrote the famous letter to his cousin Robert, reproaching him for leaving the Cistercians and going to Cluny. On this occasion Bernard compared the two ways of life in a manner which was entirely on the side of Cîteaux, and very critical of Cluny.[6] He states explicitly in this letter, that until then he had done nothing at which Cluniacs might take exception,[7] but from the time the contents of the letter became known he would be accused of slandering Cluny. In a letter written to Simon, abbot of Saint-Nicholas-aux-Bois, explaining why he had refused to accept a monk of this monastery into Clairvaux,[8] he demonstrated his good will toward the Order. Later, when Bernard came to write his *Apologia*, he will recall this fact.[9]

It was about this time, spring or perhaps the start of summer, that Bernard received a communication from William, abbot of St Thierry in the diocese of Rheims. The letter itself is no longer extant, but we do have Bernard's reply:

> I am quite prepared to undertake the task you have enjoined on me for the removal of scandal from God's kingdom, but at the moment I cannot quite see how you would like it done. I have read and reread your beautiful letter—with ever more enjoyment, since it does not pall with repetition—and I understand that you want me to convince those who complain that we are slandering the Order of Cluny, that the malicious tale which they believe and spread abroad is not true. However, it

5. *Letter* 89, 3; PL 182:221; trans. B. S. James, *The Letters of St. Bernard of Clairvaux* (London: Burns & Oates, 1953), no. 92, p. 138. Cf. *S. Bernardi Opera*, III, p. 4.
6. See D. van den Eynde, "Les premiers écrits de S. Bernard" in Leclercq, *Recueil d'études sur saint Bernard et ses écrits* (Rome: Edizioni di Storia e Letteratura, 1968), III, pp. 396ff.
7. *Letter* 1, 11; PL 182:76; trans. James, no. 1, p. 7.
8. *Letter* 84; PL 182:205; trans. James, no. 86, p. 124.
9. *Infra*, no. 4.

seems contradictory to me, having done just this, to turn round and condemn their excesses in food and clothing and the other areas you mention. Perhaps I could say first that the Order itself is quite praiseworthy, and that those who censure it should themselves be censured, and then go on to condemn the excesses present in it. Tell me frankly if this is what you want, or whether you think a different approach is called for. Do not hesitate to tell me what you want, and I shall do it. At the same time you should be aware that I find this sort of writing rather distasteful. It means a great loss of devotion and an interruption of prayer, especially when one has neither the skill nor the leisure for writing.[10]

Some have thought that this letter forms a preface to the *Apologia*, but this is not so. The letter is interesting though, because like Bernard's prefaces, it offers us a glimpse into the mind of its author. It informs us that Bernard is writing at William's request, or rather on his orders, and that its purpose is the serious one of putting an end to a scandal in God's kingdom. The charge that the Cistercians were slandering Cluny must be refuted, and the laxity which had become accepted at Cluny must be denounced. Bernard agreed that such a work was desirable. He knew also that he had something to say on this matter and that he had the prestige and competence to do so. At the same time he could not quite see how such a task could be done without making matters worse, or without contradicting himself. Could he praise the Cluniacs first, and then denounce them? His dilemma was not merely on the literary plane; religious and moral values also were involved. To solve this problem Bernard asks prayers and clarification. He himself would rather have written nothing, since he was a busy man, and he preferred to spend in prayer whatever leisure he had. We have no grounds for doubting the sincerity of this reluctance; it is in fact to the credit of this great monk.

William's reply must have smoothed matters out, for Bernard set about writing the tract. He dedicated it to William, since it was at his command that he was writing. He explained to his readers

---

10. *Letter* 84*bis*, *S. Bernardi Opera*, III, p. 64.

how the seriousness of the situation had overcome his natural repugnance for the task, and how he found himself with no alternative but to take up the pen and write as best he could. It was distasteful for him since it was no business of the monk to set himself up as judge. Jerome had written in this respect: "From our holes in the ground and our cells, we pass judgment on the world."[11] Bernard knew that he would be the object of the same sort of sarcasm if he did not do something about it. He alludes to the passage—but without mentioning Jerome by name—in the hope that alert readers might catch the reminiscence and realize that the paradox had not escaped his attention. He then outlines the scope of the tract, saying nothing, however, about his attitude to Cluny's shortcomings. In this way he tries to soften up the Black Monks. It is not very difficult to imagine their glee on a first reading, to find their adversaries so convincingly rebuked.

Then Bernard got down to work, and sometime in the summer he was able to send Oger a rough draft. Oger acknowledged receiving it, and wrote that he had compiled a preface from some of Bernard's letters, and that he had made a copy of the draft and sent it to William of St Thierry.[12] Bernard replied that this was not quite what he had intended; at the same time he admitted that he did not mind, since William was such a close friend. The text of Bernard's letter runs as follows:

> That other booklet I lent you, I had meant you only to read, but you tell me that you have had it copied. What use that can serve or whom it can possibly benefit is your responsibility. I did not intend that you should send it to the abbot of St Thierry, but I do not mind. Why should I mind his seeing it when I would gladly lay bare my whole soul for him to see if I could. . . . Do not hesitate, I beg you, to find an opportunity of going to see him, and do not, on any account, allow anyone to see or copy the aforesaid booklet until you have been through it with him, discussed it with him, and have both made such corrections as

11. Jerome, *Letter* 17, 2; C.S.E.L. 64, p. 71; trans. W. H. Fremantle, *Nicene and Post-Nicene Fathers*, second series, vol. VI, p. 21.
12. Van den Eynde, *op. cit.*, p. 399.

B

may be necessary that every word of it may be supported by two witnesses. I leave to you both to decide whether the preface you have put together out of my other letters will stand, or whether it would not be better to compose another.[13]

The following facts can be deduced from this letter: 1) Bernard had sent Oger a draft of the *Apologia* to read, but not to copy. 2) Oger had made a copy of it on his own initiative, and sent it to William of St Thierry. 3) Bernard did not disapprove of this. 4) He asked Oger to go over the text thoroughly with William, to discuss it and amend it, and to decide whether the brief preface (*praefatiuncula*) Oger had compiled was suitable, or whether something else was called for.

This raises both literary and psychological problems. In the first place, why did Bernard not send the draft to his friend, at whose instigation he was writing the *Apologia*, instead of to Oger with whom he was, to say the least, on much less familiar terms?

The answer can be found at the psychological level. It may be inferred from Bernard's letter to William that the abbot of Clairvaux was worried about the outcome of his intervention, and afraid of the reactions it might provoke. Accordingly, it is possible that he thought it a wise plan to submit the text to someone before publishing it, someone who was quite sympathetic to him, yet not so involved as William in the Cistercian-Cluniac controversy.

Is the text Bernard sent to Oger extant? There is no sign of it among the manuscripts; nor is this surprising, inasmuch as it was only a preliminary draft, not intended for publication.

Toward the end of the tract Bernard apologizes for having to bring his remarks to a precipitate conclusion: "I am prevented from going on by the burdens of my office, and by your imminent departure, dear brother Oger. You will not agree to stay any longer, and you refuse to go without this latest little book."[14] This quotation together with its context are part of the definitive text of the *Apologia*, but it was absent from the draft Bernard sent to

---

13. *Letter* 88, 3; PL 182:213; trans. James, no. 91, pp. 136f.
14. *Infra*, no. 30.

Oger, and Oger had transmitted to William. Letter eighty-eight was written after this had happened. At that stage Oger had not yet paid his visit to Clairvaux, and Bernard was not sure whether he was coming at all. It is impossible, therefore, that the draft sent to Oger includes this passage which implies that Oger was at Clairvaux for the writing of the definitive text.

Having listened to the comments of Oger and William, Bernard brings the first edition of the *Apologia* to an end. This, however, is not the conclusion of its textual development. During the summer, William asked Bernard to send him a brief preface, *praefatiuncula*, since the *Apologia* did not have one. Bernard replied that he had considered it unnecessary and had not written one.[15]

Manuscript evidence shows that the *Apologia* underwent further revision after the publication of the first edition. It is possible that William of St Thierry had offered some further suggestions on how to improve the text, as he did in the case of Bernard's tract against Abelard.[16] This first edition can be distinguished from the definitive edition by the following characteristics:

1) In chapter eight a long passage running from "For this kind of mercy . . ." in number sixteen to the beginning of number eighteen is not included.

2) In chapter nine there is a significant modification of a few phrases in number twenty-one.

3) Again in chapter nine, the whole of number twenty-two and some of number twenty-three are absent.

4) There are more than sixty variant readings of no great importance, beginning with *si quid* and *non ut*, instead of *si qua* and *non quia*, in the opening lines, and continuing through to the omission of *Deo auctore* and *ipso protectore* toward the end.

5) There are no section divisions, either by paragraph headings or by rubrics inserted in the text itself.

15. *Letter* 85, 4; PL 182:209; trans. James, no. 87, p. 127.
16. I have tried to show this in two articles: "Les formes successives de la lettre-traité de s. Bernard contre Abélard" in *Revue bénédictine*, 78 (1968), pp. 87–105, and "Les lettres de Guillaume de Saint-Thierry," which will be published in *Revue bénédictine*, 79 (1969).

Taken collectively, these variants point to a primitive edition of the text of the *Apologia* which was shorter and less polished than the one we have. The idea of the second edition was not to correct the first, as though it were faulty, but to improve it and to sharpen the nuances of its formulas. An example of this can be found in number twenty-one, where a phrase is eliminated which refers to the fact that Bernard himself had seen the abuses he was describing in the refectory at Cluny. An equivalent phrase, added in number twenty-two is very much milder. On the other hand, the two long insertions mentioned above serve only to reinforce the theme the *Apologia* has been developing all the while. These changes are much the same as those found in the two authentic editions of the sermons *On the Song of Songs*,[17] and the sermons on Psalm 90.[18]

All the variant readings proper to the first edition are itemized in the apparatus of the critical edition of the text. Here it is sufficient to say that there are not many manuscripts that follow the primitive version. This can be explained by the fact that it was only provisional, and would shortly be replaced by the definitive text. The copies we have could derive either from the original that Bernard gave to Oger, or from a copy William had at St Thierry, and which went with him to Signy. It is fairly probable that we do not possess all the copies that were made of the primitive version, though, judging from the ones we have, it seems that it never enjoyed a very wide circulation. All the ancient manuscripts which follow it, as well as the later ones with the exception of the one from Echarlis are to be found in the north of France, round the area where William and Oger had lived. Oger was a canon of Mont-Saint-Eloi in the diocese of Arras, but in 1125 he became abbot of St Médard at Tournai. The text crossed into England by way of Fécamp, which is in the diocese of Rouen, not far from Arras. Steinfeld is near Bonn, but between 1121 and 1135 this house of canons regular of the Springiersbach observance was attached by Evervin to the abbey of Prémontré, which was in the diocese of Laon, not far from Signy and St Thierry, and from which

17. Cf. *Recueil*, I (1962), pp. 329ff.
18. *Ibid.*, vol. III.

Steinfeld could easily have received its copy. Oger himself was a canon regular, and according to Vacandard,[19] he was rather proud of his correspondence with Bernard, and was glad of the opportunity to spread abroad the text of the *Apologia*, especially among his fellow canons.[20]

What title did the *Apologia* have in its first and second editions? St Bernard himself describes the work as an *apologia* in Letter eighteen.[21] In the *Vita Prima*, Geoffroy of Auxerre uses the term *Apologeticus*,[22] and in fact it is this title that is used most frequently by the manuscripts, especially the older ones, though *Liber Apologeticus* and *Apologia*, which Bernard himself used, are common enough. There is a whole group of English manuscripts, several of which are quite old, which call the tract the *Epistola de discreta varietate ordinis monastici, et de non iudicando alterius servos, et de superfluitate monachorum* (a letter on the different varieties to be found within the monastic order, on not judging another's servants, and on the excesses of monks). In a few isolated instances the tract is given a generic title, such as *Epistola de vita monastica*.[23]

Most of the manuscripts divide the different sections of the tract by means of headings or *capitula*. One set of these, which comprises ten headings altogether and is attested to by the oldest manuscripts of all regions, has been included in the critical edition of the text and in the present translation.

The overhauling of the first edition was completed toward the end of 1125, about the same time that Peter the Venerable published his defense of the monks of Cluny.[24] The question is, did Bernard have a chance to read this tract before he published his own? The

---

19. *Vie de S. Bernard* (Paris: Lecoffre, 1895), I, p. 190.

20. Details concerning the manuscript tradition of the *Apologia* will be found in the introduction to the critical edition, *S. Bernardi Opera*, III, pp. 67–69.

21. *Letter* 18, 5; PL 182:122; trans. James, no. 19, p. 54.

22. *Vita Prima S. Bernardi*, III, 29; PL 185:320.

23. Cf. *S. Bernardi Opera*, III, pp. 73–74. Also, *Recueil*, II (1966), pp. 123–126.

24. This is Letter 28 in G. Constable's edition, *The Letters of Peter the Venerable*, I (Cambridge, Mass.: Harvard University Press, 1967), pp. 52–101. On the "character" of this letter, cf. *ibid.*, II, pp. 270–274.

possibility is not be be excluded, but if he did, he did not allow it to influence his own presentation in any way, either because he wanted to avoid a personal conflict with the abbot of Cluny, or because the tract arrived too late to make any difference. At any rate, the two major contributions to the debate made their appearance at about the same time.

This was not the end of the trouble. Among the various contributions which appeared, there were two direct replies to St Bernard's charges. The first is the *Riposte* attributed to Hugh of Reading and dated 1127–1128.[25] The other is an anonymous work found in an Oxford manuscript placed immediately after the *Apologia*.[26] This second text, unlike the *Riposte*, is not addressed personally to Bernard, nor does it mention him by name or quote him. The author does not dwell on matters of peripheral importance, like food and drink and clothing; he goes straight to the heart of the question and tries to show that there is a place for a religious order which takes account of ordinary human weakness, and which sets more store by prayer than by austerity. It is more profound and more far-reaching than Hugh of Reading's sparkling reply, but in both cases the concern is the same; to defend the honor of a form of monastic life that is followed by the vast majority of monks.

Form and content

In the *Apologia* Bernard wrote with great artistry, making use of a number of literary devices of which the reader must be aware if he is to interpret the tract correctly and have some insight into the mentality of its author.

The tract is divided into two major sections of about the same length. Its development is modeled on the ancient rhetorical ploy

25. Published by Dom André Wilmart, *op. cit.* Cf. C. H. Talbot, "The Date and Author of the *Riposte*" in *Petrus Venerabilis, 1156–1956*, pp. 72–80, where the authorship and date suggested by Wilmart are confirmed.

26. I have published this under the title "Nouvelle réponse du monachisme ancien aux critiques des cisterciens" in *Receuil*, II, p. 69.

whereby an advocate begins his defense by denigrating his client; it is only when the accused is thoroughly discredited in the sight of all that he begins to rehabilitate him and eventually establish his innocence. These tactics were well known among the ancients, and are found occasionally in later writers, Shakespeare for example.[27] The Black Monks are delighted to hear their Cistercian critics rebuked, but when Bernard swings round to attack the Cluniacs, they find themselves losing favor irretrievably. In his denunciation Bernard makes use of several technical devices, such as the *praeteritio* and the *attestatio rei visae*.[28] One instance of the latter was so powerful that Bernard felt constrained to temper it when he was revising the first edition.[29]

It should be noted that although the *Apologia* looks like a case for the defense, it is really satire. Toward the end of the tract, Bernard shows that he has in mind the correction, not only of the Cluniacs, but also of those of stricter life who had become slanderers. After drawing together the threads of his argument he returns to this point at the end, showing that he is indeed thinking of both parties: "This is what I think about your Order and ours" (No. 31).

From beginning to end, therefore, the *Apologia* is written strictly according to plan. Its structure is indicated not only by the paragraph headings, but also by transitional passages of which the one that marks the break between the two major divisions takes up a whole paragraph (No. 15).

Within the two main sections there is a logical development from

27. *The Merchant of Venice*, act 4, scene 1; *Julius Caesar*, act 3, scene 2.
28. A. Forcellini defines *praeteritio* as "a rhetorical device by which we say that we are unwilling to speak of some matter and that we intend to omit reference to it altogether, and then go on to speak of it at length" (*Totius latinitatis lexicon* [London, 1828], II, p. 249). There are examples of *attestatio* in the *Apologia*, nos. 21 and 27. The term *videas*, which begins a clause in no. 21, has many parallels, e.g. Sermon 24 on the Song of Songs, nos. 3 and 4 (*S. Bernardi Opera*, I, p. 153, §8; p. 155, §14; trans. A. Luddy, *St. Bernard's Sermons on the Canticle of Canticles* [Dublin: Browne & Nolan, 1920]). On this, see L. Arbusow, *Colores Rhetorici* (Göttingen, 1948), p. 120, no. 19, "Die 'Cernes'-Formel," with examples of expressions beginning with *videas* and *cernes*.
29. Cf. *infra*, pp. 24f.

generic and doctrinal considerations to concrete practical problems. It may be represented schematically as follows:

A) 1–4   Bernard speaks of his own dispositions and his reasons for writing.

    5   A theological exposition on the theme of unity and plurality in the Church.

    6–9   Application to the various orders of monks.

    10–12 The universal necessity of charity.

    13–14 A warning to Cistercians not to attach more importance to observances than to the practice of humility and charity.

    15   *Transition.*

B) 16–18 Some general remarks on Cluniac observance.

    19   Comparison with ancient monasticism.

    20–23 Food.

    24–26 Clothing.

    27   The vain display of their abbots.

    28–29 The cost of their buildings.

    30–31 *Epilogue.*

Bernard realized that the tract was incomplete, that much more could be added. He takes advantage of its premature conclusion, however, to advance a few thoughts on the need for mutual frankness and charity. He begins on a confident note, but at the end he speaks solemnly of the right of everyone to tell another the truth about himself, and the duty of everyone to accept such admonitions when they come to him. In this way Bernard contrives to convert a mere literary convention into a telling lesson in sincerity.

Historians of art, literature and monasticism are especially interested in the second half, even though the other is richer in doctrine. It is possible that the first part was intended only as a preparation for the denunciations that were to follow, at least in the opinion of a twentieth-century critic. As far as he was concerned, Bernard was writing with all the skill of an orator:

He speaks in a way that might lead simple and superficial readers astray.

What form is it that has the function of concealing the meaning from the reader, or from those who hear it read?

The ancient masters of rhetoric called it "insinuation." It was used in defending a client who was so unpopular with the audience that they did not wish to hear his defense. The advocate of the accused began by taking sides with the opposition. Later on, by a skillful maneuvering of words he switches sides and begins to attack what he had helped to build up, and shows him to be innocent whom he had at first condemned.[30]

The fact is that Bernard's expressions of regard for Cluny, and his denunciation of its enemies served to heighten the effect of his diatribe against its abuses. With such a preparation, the attack strikes home more surely, and when the reader puts down the tract, his impression is determined almost exclusively by the invective. Everything—even Bernard's praise of Cluny, sincere though it was—contributes to make the *Apologia* a real lampoon, and its author's mastery of language assured that it would be a tremendous success.

The literary genre

Two things must be considered to arrive at a just estimate of the worth of the *Apologia*. The first is the literary genre which Bernard adopted for his tract, the second is the perfection of style that he was able to give it.

It was unthinkable for ancient and medieval writers not to base their composition on fixed rules and models appropriate to their purpose. It is these that determine the literary genre.[31]

30. *Dialogus inter Cluniacensem Monachum et Cisterciensem de Diversis utriusque Ordinis Observantiis,* Martène and Durrand, *Thesaurus Novorum Anecdotorum,* V, col. 1577. On *insinuatio,* cf. *Rhethor. ad Herenn.,* I, VI, 9.

31. I have devoted a chapter in *The Love of Learning and the Desire for God* (New York: Fordham University Press, 1961) to the subject of literary genres in monastic authors (ch. 8, pp. 153–188).

Dom André Wilmart, a very able judge of medieval Latin literature, describes the *Apologia* as a *vrai chef-d'oeuvre du genre pamphletaire.*[32] This fearless controversialist, he continues, has produced a work "more like satire than not, for there is scarcely any other word to describe the vigor of such outrageous sarcasm."[33] Did Bernard's contemporaries think the same? The only contender on the Cluniac side to refute the charges of the *Apologia* in detail, as far as we know, was the author of the *Riposte.* He states his case brilliantly and with a great deal of sincerity, and in the opinion of unbiased judges, sustains it successfully. He does not disguise his admiration for Bernard, but he does regret the tone in which he wrote. Twice in the work he describes the *Apologia* as satire.[34] Another monk of the same century gives the function of satire as reprimand: *satira propter reprehensionem.*[35]

Satire or diatribe is a bequest from ancient literary tradition. It is designedly a work in which harsh things are said in order that good may result,[36] a matter in which it is easy to go too far. As Horace himself wrote, "There are some people who say my satire is far too severe, that it goes beyond all reasonable limits. . . ."[37] Even though there is no actual untruth in the satire, exaggeration is almost inevitable; it is part of the game.[38] To condemn its use in the *Apologia* the author of the *Riposte* had only to recall Persius and Juvenal, especially as Bernard had quoted the former, framing his very words.[39] The critic is correct when he says that Bernard is using irony,[40] enjoying himself by writing seriously about things

32. "A real masterpiece of the pamphlet style"—refers to a literary style characterized by its brevity and satire. The pamphlet has been used by many famous authors to put a point across on a subject of current interest. Jonathan Swift is perhaps the best-known to English readers.

33. *Riposte*, pp. 298–299.

34. Ed. Wilmart, *ibid.*, l. 8, p. 309; l. 507, p. 322.

35. *Ibid.*, p. 303, note 2.

36. Estienne defines satire as *carmen maledicum ad carpenda hominum vitia.* Cf. *Thesaurus Linguae Latinae* (Basle, 1743), IV, p. 169.

37. *Satire*, II, i, 1–2.

38. *Riposte*, l. 55–56, p. 318; the word *exaggeratio* occurs in l. 1015, p. 335.

39. *Apologia*, no. 22, quotes Persius, *Satire*, II, 69.

40. *Riposte*, l. 947–949, p. 334.

that are really funny.[41] For example, in his remarkable description of Cluniac egg cookery, Bernard exhibits an extraordinary sense of the comic and doubtlessly won an easy laugh.[42] The copiers entered into his mood and bolstered his formulas in various ways. One of them even added a new item to the list of egg-dishes. Bernard had written: "They might be fried or roasted or stuffed," and the copier added *nunc mollia*, "they might be cooked soft." He was a Norman, and it may be that he had read the *Riposte*, which was most probably written by Hugh of Reading, a French monk in England. The *Riposte* also mentions the matter of soft or hard eggs, *mollia aut dura*,[43] which were the masterpieces of the Cluniac kitchens. The additions in the Fécamp manuscript would therefore be explained by a reminiscence of the text of the *Riposte*.

The picture of gluttons stuffed so full of exotic foods that they cannot take any more is commonplace in satire. In general the authors of the gastronomic poems seem to develop the same themes, the search for bizarre and unusual foods, the cooking until it is "just right," the fine art of sauce-concoction, which is so important because it is a means of transforming the natural taste of the food.[44]

Monastic authors treating of such banquets follow the same general pattern. Long before the *Apologia* Peter Damian penned the following vigorous passage:

> It has displeased me a great deal to see the way monks in many monasteries behave. They are in excellent health, without the slightest need for medical care, yet today they will have a physician let blood, tomorrow they will be using swallows, and then every day will see them with some new remedy. Meanwhile the wheat must be ground fine, and cakes gently cooked for them over ashes. The rivers and the seas must be combed, and there is no let-up for the markets, the ocean's depths are being emptied

41. *Ibid.*, l. 684, p. 327.
42. *Ibid.*, l. 408, p. 320.
43. *Ibid.*, l. 434–437, p. 320.
44. Horace, *Sat.*, II, viii, 28: *longe dissimilem noto celantia sucum.* Cf. *Sat.* II, iv, 38, 40–50, 63–64.

of fish. The fact that the supply of fish has ceased is regarded as an unfortunate mishap, for a heavy demand leads to new sources and new sources lead to greater needs. Meanwhile every living thing on land and sea is brought to slaughter, and it is time to look round for a suitable cook. He must be one who has a knack of controlling the fire so that the heat goes right into the bones while the flesh is not scorched; the heat must penetrate inside, but without harming the outside. What else can be said? Those who sit down to such a meal, or perhaps recline for it, feast until they are so sick to their stomach that they can eat no more. Before they were only pretending, but now they are really sick.[45]

The mild-mannered Peter the Venerable, a contemporary of St Bernard, could not resist writing a page in the same vein:

From all directions they converge, like kites or vultures they quickly make their way to wherever they detect the smoke of a kitchen fire, or their nostrils catch the smell of roasting meat. . . . They are sick of beans and cheese and eggs and even fish, all they want are the flesh-pots of Egypt. The table of holy monks is covered with pork, roasted or boiled, fat heifers, rabbits, hares and the best goose of the gaggle, chicken and every conceivable farmyard bird or beast. After a time even these lose their savor, familiarity breeds contempt. Then they are after foreign delicacies that are fit for a king. Nowadays a monk is satisfied only by venison and the flesh of such wild animals as boars and bears. Hunters must be called in to comb the forests, and fowlers to trap pheasant and partridge and turtledoves, lest the servant of God die of starvation. Take care that none of his whims is left unsatisfied, otherwise he will surely perish. . . . The estates of Cluny are not enough to provide for our lavish banquets, so that it looks as though we shall have to sell off some of the land and its appurtenances to satisfy the monks' appetites. They spend their whole time idling and feasting and preparing themselves for never-ending torments.[46]

Finally we might have a look at a passage from the *Apologia*:

45. *Opusc.* 49, 6; PL 145:726c.
46. *Letter* 161; Constable, *op. cit.*, p. 389.

At table, while the mouth is filled with food, the ears are nourished with gossip so absorbing that all moderation in eating is forgotten. Meanwhile course after course is brought in. Only meat is lacking, and to compensate for this, two huge servings of fish are given. You might have thought that the first was sufficient, but even the recollection of it vanishes, once you have started on the second. . . . Once the palate is attracted to piquant flavors, ordinary things begin to pall; but if there is question of unusual flavors, desire is as quickly aroused as if the meal had not yet begun. The selection of dishes is so exciting that the stomach does not realize that it is being overtaxed. . . . Who could describe all the ways in which eggs are tampered with or tortured, or the care that goes into turning them one way and then turning them back? They might be cooked soft, hard, or scrambled. They might be fried, roasted, and occasionally they are stuffed. Sometimes they are served with other foods, and sometimes on their own. What reason can there be for all this variation except the gratification of a jaded appetite? . . . Three or four times during a meal you might see a cup brought in, half-full, so that the different wines can be sampled, more by aroma than by taste. It is not swallowed, but only caressed, since a seasoned palate can quickly distinguish one wine from another, and select the stronger. It is even alleged to be the custom in some monasteries to give the community honeyed or spiced wine on the major feasts. Is this also on account of stomach troubles? . . . When the monk gets up from table and the swollen veins in his temple begin to throb, all he is fit for is to go back to bed. After all, if you force a man to come to the Office of Vigils before his digestion is complete, all you will extract from him is a groan instead of a tone.[47]

This is the picture of the monastic refectory independently sketched out for us by three reformers of the eleventh and twelfth centuries. Are we therefore obliged to regard their descriptions as historical accounts from which we may garner details of monastic menus for the period and locality in which they wrote? All that can be established from these three invectives is a common regard for

47. *Apologia*, nos. 20–21. With regard to the literal meaning of the texts, it is scarcely necessary to underline the discrepancy between Bernard, who grants that meat was abstained from, and Peter the Venerable, who says that it was not.

austerity, expressed in each case in the same literary form, that of satire. None of these authors could resist the pleasure of writing an effortless page of good prose. The author of the *Riposte* rather grumpily suggests that Bernard put a good deal of effort into his description of Cluniac egg cookery.[48] However, the passage in question is one of the rare parts of the *Apologia* which was left unchanged in the second edition; it was perfect from the start. The literary excellence of the tract is obtained at the expense of justice, since the reproaches are really harsher than they should have been; it is very difficult to ridicule something without going too far. This was why Hugh of Reading criticized the whole second part of the *Apologia*; he thought that Bernard should have put a curb on his talent.[49]

It is very important to know what was going on in Bernard's own mind. Dom Wilmart, who was so harsh in his condemnation of the general tone of the *Apologia*, is very understanding when he comes to examine Bernard's intentions. "St. Bernard," he writes, "was a sort of visionary who instinctively set himself on a plane higher than that of immediate realities, who used to walk past people without even noticing them. In the same way he was able to give offense without being aware of it."[50] The only explanation one can offer is to point to Bernard's own zeal, his love for perfection, and his impatience with mediocrity; he wished that all monks would attain the loftiest heights of austerity. There is a certain amount of unreality in such an aspiration, which means that his criticisms were unfair to some degree. Even this is only the darker side of something that is essentially positive. Hugh of Reading took all the jibes of the *Apologia* rather seriously, but Bernard and William of St Thierry were not fooled by them: they knew them for what they were. The author of the *Riposte* was right to stand up for Cluny's reputation; he also had a high regard for his own Order. He was right on a literary level; if the *Apologia* wishes to paint a picture of monastic behavior, it is false and inaccurate. But on the plane

48. *Riposte*, l. 415–422, p. 320.   49. *Ibid.*, l. 743f., p. 327.
50. *Ibid.*, p. 298, note 4.

of the spiritual, which was Bernard's natural habitat, the *Apologia* rings true. The literary skill which Bernard lavished on the tract is only a means of expressing an ideal, for which monks of all ages should be grateful. In fact it was the Black Monks, the object of his attack, who were most instrumental in spreading his writings,[51] so well aware were they of the extraordinary combination of holiness and literary talent which these works embody.

The exaggerations to be found in the *Apologia* were no more than one would expect to find in a satire; both Bernard and his readers understood this. Dom Mège, a solemn Maurist of the seventeenth century, felt obliged to counter Bernard's description of the different ways of cooking eggs, with the observation that St Benedict had allowed two cooked dishes at each meal, "so that those who cannot eat one can make their meal on the other."[52] This is hardly necessary. It is better to let the matter pass with a smile, and concentrate on catching Bernard's lesson on simplicity and austerity. The indignation proper to the satirical author likewise explains his impassioned tone. The descriptions of the Cluniac at table or his abbot on a trip are not meant to be more factual than the twelve proud men who people the second part of *The Steps of Humility*. E. Faral's remark on this matter is excellent:

The rhetoric of the ancients included description among the means by which an orator was able to persuade or move his audience. This view was widely held in the Middle Ages. When an author produced a descriptive passage, his aim was to act on the sensibilities and the imagination of his reader. Virtually none of the medieval authors, in Latin or vernacular, described things for the mere pleasure of definition or demonstration or to convey an objective picture of things. This is why people go astray when they try to find in them a faithful and meaningful portrayal of things and events that exist no longer. The fact is that neither historians not archeologists will find them particularly

---

51. I have given some details on the role played by Benedictines in the circulation of St Bernard's writings in *Receuil*, II, pp. 19–34, 141–148.

52. *Rule*, ch. 39, 4. Dom Mège, *Commentaire sur la Règle de S. Benoît* (Paris, 1687), p. 534.

instructive, since their whole concern was to stir up emotional reactions in the souls of their readers.[53]

Within the limits of the literary genre he had adopted, the themes Bernard developed were monastic. For example, his protests against sculpture and other images inside the monastery were part of a long monastic tradition going back to Cassian.[54] His indignation at the immensity of some of the buildings he encountered can be paralleled in the writings of reformers of every age,[55] and also in hagiography.[56] His allusion to Cluniac wine-sampling has many precedents.[57] Consider Bernard's description of the church at Cluny: "I shall say nothing about the soaring heights, and extravagant lengths and unnecessary widths of the churches, nothing about their expensive decorations and their novel images. . . ."[58] Here we see Bernard making use of three rhetorical devices. The first

53. E. Faral, "Sidoine Apollinaire et la technique littéraire du moyen âge" in *Miscellanea Giovanni Mercati* (Vatican City: Polyglot Press, 1946), vol. II, p. 568.

54. Cassian, *Conferences*, X, 5; C.S.E.L. 13, pp. 10–16; trans. C. S. Gibson in *Nicene and Post-Nicene Fathers*, second series, vol. XI, p. 403. On Cassian and others as sources of St Bernard's use of *acedia*, see S. Wenzel, "Acedia in 1100–1200" in *Traditio*, 22 (1966), pp. 86–89.

55. I have given the texts in *Aux sources de la spiritualité occidentale*, pp. 180–184.

56. In his *Life* of Eigil of Fulda, Candidus of Fulda puts into the mouth of Emperor Louis the Pious a discourse in which, citing St John Chrysostom, he advises monks henceforward to give their money to the poor instead of constructing *immensa aedificia* (ed. J. Mabillon in *Acta Sanctorum O.S.B.*, vol. IV [Venice, 1735], i, p. 223, note 11). See also *Monumenta Germaniae Historiae*, *SS.*, XV, 226–227. On this latter text, see J. Semmler in *Corpus consuetudinum monasticarum* (Sieburg, 1964), vol. I, p. 230. In William of Malmesbury's *Life of St Wulstan*, the development of the theme is summarized by Mabillon in a marginal note: *Modestus in aedificiis, etiam sacris*; *op. cit.*, VI, ii, pp. 835f.

57. *Apologia*, no. 21. The first edition had read: *vina dum potando ac probando potantur*. Hugeburge's *Life of St Wunibald* has: *Parvum vini potum utere solebat, ut iam pene non bibendo, sed probando, maiores patiebat gustando continentiam quam aliter non recipiendo* (*Monumenta Germaniae Historiae, SS.*, VI, iii, 7–8). The expression that Hugeburge of Heidenheim uses to connote abstemiousness, Bernard uses to indicate excess. Cf. Geoffrey of Vinsauf's expression *nec vina probans*, in *Poetrio nova* (c. 1793), quoted by Faral, *op. cit.*, p. 574.

58. *Apologia*, no. 28. Other examples of such accumulation of epithets are found in Faral, *op. cit.*, pp. 574ff.

is the *praeteritio*, which involves affirming one's reluctance to speak about the matter at issue.[59] The second is the accumulation of epithets, *immensas altitudines, immoderatas longitudines, supervacuas latitudines, sumptuosas depolitiones, curiosas depolitiones.* Finally, there is his use of assonance, well controlled since he realizes that too much of it can become tiresome. In the passage which speaks of "the mingling of harmony and discord" in the Church, there is a distinct possibility that Bernard is repeating a formula of Ovid.[60] Bernard illustrates the theme of diversity in unity by recourse to Jn 14:2, "In my Father's house there are many rooms." An examination of St Augustine's commentary on this verse reveals that Bernard has certainly been inspired by it when writing the *Apologia*.[61] There are the same ideas, several parallel formulas, and the same reference to 1 Cor 15:41, "Star differs from star in glory." To gauge the familiar liberty the abbot of Clairvaux allowed himself in the use of his source, one only has to compare the *Apologia* with the tract *De diversis ordinibus Ecclesiae*.[62] The author develops the same theme and uses the same sources, but he lacks wealth of biblical imagery that Bernard has added to Augustine, and which makes the *Apologia* at once more striking and more lyrical.

The style of the Apologia

One thing we do know for certain about the *Apologia* is that Bernard took great pains in its composition. He submitted it to the

59. See note 28.
60. *Metamorph.*, I, 432–433.
    Cumque sit ignis aquae pugnax, vapor umidus omnes
      Recreat et discors concordia fetibus apta est.
Bernard's text read: *intelligens denique Ecclesia hanc suam quodammodo discordem concordiam concerdemve discordiam.*

61. St Augustine, *In Joannem*, 67, 2–3; *Corp. Christ.*, no. 36, pp. 495f.; trans. J. Gibb and J. Innes in *Nicene and Post-Nicene Fathers*, first series, vol. VII, pp. 321f.

62. *De diversis ordinibus Ecclesiae*, I; PL 213:813. The author seems to have been Rimbaud, a canon regular of Liège, writing between 1125 and 1130. This is C. Dereine's opinion: "Les origines de Prémontré" in *Rev. d'hist. ecclés.*, 42 (1947), pp. 359–360, 376–377.

C

examination of his two friends, and then re-worked it before bringing it to completion. Since we have the original text which was
privately circulated and the edition that Bernard eventually
published, we are able to compare the two and discover what
Bernard had in mind when he made the alterations.

From the start the *Apologia* was written with great verve. The
revision of the text only increased its vigor. Sixty-four corrections
were involved altogether, not counting insufficiently attested
variants that can be traced to copiers' errors. Nearly every page has
one or two changes, at an average frequency of one every ten lines.
What is the point in such changes? Often it is hard to tell. Why,
for example, did Bernard replace *si* quid *me scriptitare iussistis* and
non ut *negligerem* by *si* qua *me scriptitare iussistis* and *non* quia *negligerem?* The author made these subtle changes when rereading the
text months later, and it is not always possible for us to work out
why. We are not aware of any improvement in grammar, content
or rhythm, since we are not able to read the text with the accent,
intonation and pronunciation that his contemporaries used, much
less with his own. Bernard's intentions in making these revisions
remain his own secret. Most of the corrections are small. The word
order is changed nine times, either to improve the sound of it, or
to bring out a nuance or heighten a contrast between two words.

It is fairly easy to go through the critical edition of the *Apologia*
and draw up a list of all the corrections and then classify them as
grammatical, rhythmic, or stylistic. Such facts are a means of
studying Bernard's methods of composition. For the moment it is
sufficient to say that the changes rarely modify the meaning of the
passage concerned. In one place the abbot of Clairvaux eliminates
a phrase which had underlined the fact that he had been an eye-
witness to the abuses he was describing. He replaced, "It is embarrassing to speak of such things that, had I not seen them with
my own eyes, I would scarcely have credited," with "It is embarrassing to speak of these things, but it should be more embarrassing
still to do them. If you are ashamed to hear them mentioned, you
needn't be too ashamed to amend." The second expression is even
more severe than the first, but its substitution at least forestalled

the criticism that Bernard was ungrateful for the hospitality he had received at Cluny. Most of the other minor corrections tell us less about what was going on in Bernard's mind than about his exactitude in the choice of language. This trait is often under-estimated, but it is really very revealing.

Apart from the less important changes, Bernard introduced two new passages in his second edition. The second of these is simply inserted in the text without requiring any modifications. The other passage required a few slight changes in the paragraph that followed it. Here, as in Sermons twenty-four and seventy-one on the *Song of Songs*, in the prologues to the *Sermons on Psalm ninety*, and the *Sermons in Praise of the Virgin Mary*, the seam is imperceptible. Bernard was, as he admitted, a master of "invisible mending" (*resarcire*).

Both the additions are in the second part. There is no tempering of his invective. In the first Bernard denounces with a series of scriptural texts the illusion that allowed laxity to pass itself off as discretion. The second introduces some new material which Bernard had not foreseen when drawing up the original plan. Apparently he had picked up some details which he had not known before. It was reported to him that there were hale and hearty young monks who had transferred to the infirmary for the sole purpose of qualifying for the mitigations allowed the sick, notwith-standing the fact that the Cluniac regime was never particularly severe. To earn their places at the better laden tables these monks had to support a pretense of illness with the aid of walking sticks, so that it might look as though they were exhausted. "Should we laugh or cry at such foolishness?"

Finally, when reading any of St Bernard's writings we must take note of the individual nature of each. His own contemporaries were able to do this more readily than we, since we have lost contact with classical literary tradition. The *Apologia* is not a factual document meant to convey details of the actual state of Cluniac observance. It is a caricature, designed to correct them. There is a certain amount of sarcasm and exaggeration, and it is always poss-ible that these be carried too far—though this is not the case in the present instance—but even so, it is a legitimate method of composition, and we must not allow ourselves to be led astray by it. Bernard is only one of many who have developed the theme of the fantastic feast, though he does it rather well, and in his own particular style. He has no intention of giving an objective analysis of the Cluniac diet; he merely gives an amusing lesson in the demands of monastic austerity. In the various monasteries where this tract was found, it is probably true to say that the monks were grateful to St Bernard for making his spirituality so entertaining.

The contemporary relevance of the Apologia

We have already discussed St Bernard's teaching in the *Apologia*, and the classical, biblical, patristic, and monastic sources he followed. With Bernard there is no separation of content from literary expression; he is at one and the same time a theologian and an artist, and style was as much part of his writing as the truth he expounded.

All that remains to be done is to indicate briefly the dominant themes of the *Apologia*, the key ideas which allow us to catch hold of its message. These have to do with Christ, monasticism as a way of Christian life, the role of monasticism in the life of the Church, and the way monastic life should be lived.

As usual Bernard's approach is Christocentric. He speaks of seeking only Christ, hoping in him alone (No. 1), of carrying his cross, sharing in his suffering, and imitating his humility (No. 2), poverty (No. 3), and obedience (No. 6), so as to share his joy in the present life and his glory in the next. Bernard insists very strongly throughout the *Apologia* on poverty and he treats of it at length toward the end (No. 28). This alone is sufficient to give the tract some importance for Christians of today. Poverty is understood in its deeper meaning, as it is embodied in Christ, who is its origin and model.[63] Over and above the rejection of superfluities, this

63. I have given various biblical and patristic texts on this point in *Aspects of Monasticism, Yesterday and Today* (Cistercian Studies Series 7), ch.3.

virtue involves the renunciation of all personal privilege, self-complacence, superiority, pride and self-satisfaction. In the *Apologia* Bernard recalls the teaching of Jesus on simplicity of heart as opposed to hypocrisy, pharisaism, and judgment of others which is not based on concern for their welfare (Nos. 10–11); on inwardness (No. 12), as well as the superiority of heartfelt love and purity of intention over all outward observance (Nos. 13–14).

Such love, which is God, comes from the Father, is made manifest in the Son, and was communicated by the Holy Spirit to the monks of old, the Fathers of monastic life. It was from them that monasticism began; they invented it, they were its begetters. It might be said that they were the channels by which the Holy Spirit was communicated to their followers. A monk has only to look back to their charisms, their experience, their example, their teaching, to the ideal that has always found expression in the Church. This is why Bernard insists on a fidelity to the holy founders—either those of primitive monasticism or those of more recent times (Nos. 4, 19, 23). This too is very much to the point in these days when Vatican II has asked all religious to do precisely what Bernard recommends.

At the same time, Bernard does not set any one of them up as an absolute model. It is collectively that their example has validity. Their common ideal finds different expressions which are all legitimate insofar as they are both effects and signs of the mystery of the one Church of Jesus Christ. Today there is much talk about pluralism. The idea is not new, and it has never been formulated so powerfully and at such length and with such artistry as in the passage of the *Apologia* where Bernard justifies—or rather admires and praises—the diversity of observances to be found within a single ideal. The love of Christ always present in the Church is the life of the Church; it never ceases to promote the growth of the Church and to raise up new forms of life in the Holy Spirit. This continual growth is the means by which the Church maintains its steady progress toward full maturity. It is an eschatological anticipation of the life of the heavenly city that Bernard portrays, drawing on the Book of Revelation, St Paul, and the Prophets. This vision of

the Church, charged as it is with biblical poetry, draws from
Bernard pages which are as beautiful as any he wrote, and which
are among the most beautiful in the entire literature of ecclesiology.

The practical teaching on monastic life in the second part is
nothing more than the embodiment of the theological principles
already enunciated. Two of the paragraph headings (Nos. 16, 24)
show that his attack is directed against superfluities, against whatever is not required by monastic life as such—as related to the hope
one has in Christ, and to one's love for him, which enables a man
to give up whatever does not contribute to the realization of this
ideal, and even more so whatever impedes it. Hence discretion is to
be understood not as a mitigation which paves the way to an easy
life, but a new decision regarding what is consistent with the ideal,
and what is not. Such a decision will vary according to time, place,
and culture. The concrete establishing of what is superfluous and
what is not, will change, but the principle behind such a decision
is the same. Bernard applies this principle to conditions of his own
age, to food and clothing, and to the style appropriate to abbots
when abroad, and who would deny that the last point, at least, is
perennial?

There is one point to which historians attach special importance,
although it is only secondary in relation to the principles involved,
and this is Bernard's attitude toward Church art and architecture.
It is here perhaps that the exaggeration proper to satire looms
largest. Bernard's general notion is that as far as monks are concerned, beauty should be simple and unaffected, and as pure as the
God it reflects. Here we must beware of making over-facile
generalizations about Benedictine "sumptuousness" and Cistercian
"austerity." The fact is that most monastic churches are modest
enough, both in size and design. In particular, the Cluniac dependencies were unassuming, built according to the current style. By
way of exception, there were a few basilicas which were centers of
pilgrimage, like Cluny and Saint-Benoît-sur-Loire. In these their
size was increased to cater to the non-monastic purpose they ful-
filled, and their decor was often similar to that of cathedrals and
parish churches. The Cistercians wanted all their abbeys built in

out-of-the-way places, and they did not allow visitors access to their churches. This is why simplicity remained supreme.[64] However, as communities grew, the Cistercians too were obliged to erect vast monasteries which were sometimes larger and just as expensive as those built by other orders. The solid and impressive, but tremendously harmonious proportions of Fontenay, which was built according to Bernard's intentions, is one of the best examples of the style of architecture he was calling for. One curious fact is, however, that among the twelfth-century monasteries remaining today, the most modest and most in line with Bernard's ideas are not those founded from Clairvaux, but places like Senanque and Le Thoronet, which derive from Cîteaux.

Finally, to bring the *Apologia* to a close Bernard writes briefly on a subject which he will be treating in his tract, *Monastic Obligations and Abbatical Authority*, and in many of his letters; the transfer of monks from one order to another. The few remarks he makes here have to be judged in the light of his more detailed teaching, as well as his own practice in this matter.

*　　　*　　　*

Like every great work that bears the impress of genius and sanctity, the *Apologia* never grows old. It is as young and fresh and relevant today as when it was first published. To appreciate this, however, it is necessary to appreciate the double aspect of Bernard's greatness; on the one hand, his literary genius which enabled him to handle satire, humor and sarcasm with much mastery, on the other the purity of his experience of the mystery of Christ in the Church which gave him a basis for distinguishing the essential from what was peripheral. The only thing that cannot be replaced is love, everything else can and does change. If today monks could help each other in this task of discerning what is central and what is not— and this is what *aggiornamento* is all about—they would be rendering each other a service that would bear witness to their common

64. Further details on this point can be found in J. Hubert et al., *Moissac et l'occident au XIe siècle* (Toulouse, 1964), pp. 47–58.

seeking after God in humility. In this way the frankness that Bernard asks for in the last lines of the *Apologia* would be continually realized in the Church. "Whatever is praiseworthy in your monks I praise and extol. On the other hand, to you and to my other friends I point out whatever is worthy of reproach, in order that it may be corrected. This is not slander, but candor, and I ask you very earnestly, always to do the same for us."

Jean Leclercq OSB

Clervaux Abbey,
  Luxembourg

TRANSLATOR'S NOTE

Something should be said about the principles underlying the present translation. I shall merely indicate the broad lines of policy, leaving to the reader the task of assessing the extent of its application, and the validity of its premises.

It is impossible to produce an English version of the *Apologia* without a compromise of some sort. So happily married is the content of the *Apologia* to the genius of the Latin language, that a very literal translation is most undesirable. Replacing the sparkling verve of the original with a limp and prolix English rendering, would destroy the *Apologia's* eminent readability. To a large extent also, it would undermine the plausibility of Bernard's position. The *Apologia* is not primarily a logical presentation of certain basic monastic values; it is more like an appeal to the heart for their implementation. It is meant to evoke a reaction and a response in the reader. A translation fails if it reproduces the logical content in hollow isolation, incorporating nothing of the spirit or zest of the original.

In practice the best results are achieved by keeping the prose moving, by keeping it bright and brisk, and not too ponderous. This may involve the modification of sentence structure or a redistribution of elements within a period. In some cases it was desirable to replace a string of rhetorical questions with emphatic statements. Words and phrases which serve the sole function of lubricating the Latinity have been suppressed where they would impede the flow of English. It was with more regret that I allowed some precious nuances to slip away. In particular, many biblical reminiscences had to be relinquished. These scriptural undertones are so characteristic of St Bernard that it was unfortunate to lose them. In the Latin they were valuable aids in holding the reader's attention, as it were punctuating a passage with pleasant spasms of recognition. But there is no common English text today that can serve in this way. The same holds for the puns and ploys which Bernard habitually scatters through his prose. These agreeable by-products of his style must be subordinated to the primary purpose of his writing; in translation this usually means their suppression. It is unfortunate, but unavoidable.

In the notes I have tried to give something of the *Apologia's* wider context, and to clear up any misunderstandings that are liable to occur. Contrasting positions adopted by other personalities in the controversy are indicated briefly, as well as parallel passages in Bernard's other writings. The principal scriptural allusions are identified, though it must be recalled that Bernard was using the Vulgate text, which often differs substantially from our modern versions. Direct citations are translated to fit the context, though where there are alternative systems of reference (e.g. in the Psalms), I have followed the Revised Standard Version.

The translation itself is based on the critical Latin edition published by Jean Leclercq and Henri Rochais in the third volume of the *Sancti Bernardi Opera*.[1] References to other works of St Bernard are, wherever possible, to the critical edition published in this series. Otherwise they are to Mabillon's edition in Migne.[2] As far as I know this is the first complete English translation of the *Apologia;* although, it is true, Ailbe Luddy did include most of it in his *Life*

1. Rome: Editiones Cistercienses, 1963.
2. References to Bernard's works in Migne all occur in vol. 182, so I have simply cited them by column. The same holds for the writings of Peter the Venerable, which are all contained in vol. 189.

and Teaching of St Bernard.[3] For the convenience of English-speaking readers I have also referred to the best available translations of Bernard's other works.[4]

Michael Casey ocso

Tarrawarra Abbey
  Australia

3. Pp. 98–104.
4. Most of Bernard's sermons have been translated by Ailbe Luddy; *St Bernard's Sermons on the Canticle of Canticles*, 2 vols. (Dublin: Browne & Nolan, 1920). *St Bernard's Sermons for the Seasons and the Principal Festivals of the Year*, 3 vols. (Dublin: Browne & Nolan, 1921–1925). For the *De gradibus humilitatis et superbiae*, I have used the version by Geoffrey Webb and Adrian Walker, *The Steps of Humility* (London: Mowbrays, 1956). For the *Letters*, the excellent rendition by Bruno Scott James was the obvious choice; *The Letters of St Bernard of Clairvaux* (London: Burns & Oates, 1952).

AN APOLOGIA TO ABBOT WILLIAM

To the Reverend Father William,[1]
From Brother Bernard, the unworthy servant of the brothers at Clairvaux,
Greetings in the Lord.

PRIOR TO THIS, if you had asked me to do some writing, I would not have agreed, or if I had agreed, it would have been reluctantly. It is not that I care nothing for your requests, it is simply that I would never have dared to attempt something so beyond my capabilities. Now that the situation has become really serious, my former diffidence has vanished. Spurred on by the need for action, mine is the painful position of having no alternative but to comply, without worrying about how well I can do it.

How can I possibly keep quiet when I hear your complaints

---

1. William of St Thierry, at whose request the *Apologia* was written, was a close friend of St Bernard for thirty years, and the first to write his biography. He was born at Liège about 1085. After studying at Laon for some time, he entered the Benedictine Abbey of St Nicasius at Rheims. About 1120, he was elected abbot of St Thierry. In 1135 he entered the Cistercian abbey of Signy, and died there in 1148. He was the author of several works, the most famous of which is the "Golden Epistle" to the Carthusians of Mont-Dieu. Cf. Jean-Marie Déchanet, *William of Saint-Thierry, The Man and His Work,* Cistercian Studies Series 10. Louis Bouyer, *The Cistercian Heritage* (London: Mowbrays, 1958), pp. 67–124.

against us? You say that we poor men who are clothed in rags[2] dare, from our holes in the ground, as Jerome says,[3] to pass judgment on the world. You say that we insult your glorious Order,[4] and shamelessly slander the holy men who belong to it and are more deserving of our praise. You say that from our base obscurity[5] we dare to scoff at the world's luminaries. This is more unbearable still. If it is true, then under sheep's disguise we are, not ravenous wolves, but nibbling fleas and gnawing moths. We are afraid to make a public outcry, yet, with our whispered calumny we secretly eat away good men's reputations.

If this is how things stand, what will it profit us to be put to death without cause all the day long, and accounted as sheep for the slaughter?[6] If, I repeat, we are proud pharisees who look down on others, and even despise men better than ourselves, we can expect no advantage from a diet that is lean and unlovely, nor from the well-known cheapness and roughness of our clothes. The sweat of daily toil, our continual fasts and vigils, and all the austerity of our way of life will do us no good, unless it happen that we are per-

---

2. *In pannis et semicinctiis.* The first Cistercians were famous for their poor clothing. "They rejected what was contrary to the Rule, namely, wide *cucullae*, furs, linen shirts, cowls, breeches. . . ." (*Exordium Parvum*, XV; PL 166: 1507; trans. R. Larkin in Lekai, *The White Monks* [Okauchee: Cistercian Fathers, 1953], p. 262). Cf. *Exordium Magnum*, dist. I, cap. 20; [ed. Griesser (Rome: Editiones Cistercienses, 1961), p. 75, l. 25f.]. The *semicinctium* was probably some sort of loin-cloth worn underneath the robe.

3. Lit. "as *he* says." See introduction, p. 7. The reference is to Jerome's *Letter* 17, 2, C.S.E.L. 64, p. 71; trans. in *Nicene and Post-Nicene Fathers* (Grand Rapids: Eerdmans, 1957, second series, vol. VI, p. 21). Cf. Bernard's *Letter* 48, 3; PL 156c; trans. James, no. 51, p. 81).

4. St Thierry was not, in fact, affiliated to Cluny, even though Bernard speaks in no. 23 of the Fathers of Cluny as "your founders and teachers." The *Apologia* is nominally addressed to all Black Monks, though it is clear that very often Bernard is really thinking of Cluny.

5. *Umbra ignobilitatis*; Bernard often employs the term *umbra* to designate the hidden and obscure character of Cistercian monasticism. For an analysis of the theme, together with relevant bibliographical information, see Jean Leclercq, "La vie cachée" in *Chances de la spiritualité occidentale* (Paris: Cerf, 1966), pp. 279f.

6. Cf. Ps 44:22; "without cause" may derive from Ps 73:13.

forming these works with a view to being seen by men. But Christ says: "I tell you in all truth, these men have already received their reward."[7] For it is certainly true that "if we have hope in Christ in this life alone, we are the most pitiable of all men."[8] Such indeed we are, if by our service of Christ we are seeking glory only in the present life.

2. Poor remnant of a man that I am! I try so hard not to be like, or rather not to seem like the rest of men,[9] yet I will receive little for my efforts. In fact, I shall be judged more severely than anybody else. Why hasn't someone discovered a more comfortable way to hell? If we must go there, why shouldn't we join the throng which takes the broad path that leads to death? Then, at least, we could have joy instead of sorrow, before passing into that final sorrow. Oh, how much luckier are they who have no thought for death! They remain steadfast throughout their troubles. They are not upset and afflicted as other men are.[10] Even though sinners will have to suffer forever because of life's joys, at least they enjoyed plenty of the good things of this world. Oh, unhappy are they who carry a cross, not like the Savior, who carried his own, but like the Cyrenian who carried another's.[11] Unhappy the harpers who play, not on their own harps, as do the men in Revelation, but on someone else's, like

---

7. Mt 6:5.   8. 1 Cor 15:19.
9. Cf. Mt 7:13.   10. Cf. Ps 73:4f.

11. The same unfavorable interpretation of Simon's cross-bearing is found in St Bernard's sermon for the feast of St Benedict, no. 6. "Trees that bear fruit which is not their own are hypocrites; like Simon of Cyrene, they carry someone else's cross. This they do under pressure and with no religious intent since they are forced to do unpleasant things by their desire for vain-glory" (*S. Bern. Op.*, V, p. 55; trans. Luddy, *Principal Festivals*, III, pp. 122f.). The theme is treated more amply in one of the passages edited by Dom Séjourné in "Les inédits bernardins du Ms. d'Anchin" (*S. Bernard et son temps*, II [Dijon: Académie des Sciences, Artes, et Belles-Lettres, 1929], p. 270, App. A): "The fourth type of cross is the one which Simon (i.e. the obedient man) carried. He bears all the difficulties of obedience with alacrity, and carries any cross in the same way that he carried the Lord's. He runs and he works because he is under pressure from two implacable task-masters, pride and vain-glory. In the end he will not enjoy the fruit of obedience, since he will not be judged on the basis of his external obedience, but according to his internal obedience and right intention."

hypocrites.[12] Twice unhappy are they who are both proud and poor. Twice unhappy, I repeat, are those who carry Christ's cross without following after him, who share in his sufferings with no thought of imitating his humility.

3. Such people are doomed to a double measure of punishment. In the present life they punish themselves to win the world's praise; in the next, their inward pride will cause them to be thrown into unending torment. They toil with Christ, yet they will not reign with him. Though they imitate Christ in his poverty, they will not share his glory. In their journeying they drink from the stream, but they will never lift up their head in the homeland.[13] They mourn here, but hereafter they will not be comforted.[14] And rightly so. It is not for pride to deck itself out in the swaddling clothes of Jesus' humility.[15] It is true that contact with his childhood is the only remedy for human sinfulness. But what are we to think when pride squeezes itself into the Lord's crib in order to deceive, when instead of innocent whimpers, we find there the evil whispers of slander. The proud men in the Psalm,[16] whose bodies seethe with malice and who are openly adorned with ungodliness and vice are in a better position than we, who try to conceal vice under a cloak of virtue. The man who adds falsehood to his other vices by pretending to be holy, is twice as blameworthy as one who acknowledges his own defects.

Now what shall I say? I am afraid that I myself may be thought guilty on this score, not by you Father, of course, not by you. I know that you understand me as well as any man can in this land of darkness, and in this matter especially, I know that you are aware of what I think. These things that you have often heard orally from me I am committing to writing for the sake of those who do not know me as well as you do, and with whom I have not discussed

---

12. Cf. Rev 14:2.   13. Cf. Ps 110:7.   14. Cf. Mt 5:4.

15. The same metaphor occurs in *Letter* 51: "But now they are looking for simony under the swaddling clothes of the child Jesus" (PL 159a; trans. James, No. 54, p. 83).

16. Ps 73:7.

matters as I have with you. I cannot go round and explain my position to each one individually. Instead, I write this, so that you will have something from me with which to convince them on my behalf of what you yourself know quite definitely from my own lips. There is nothing in my private conversations with you on this subject, that I am afraid to lay before the eyes of all.

II. 4. No one had ever heard me denouncing this Order or murmuring against it. I am always delighted to see any of its members. I receive them with all due honor; I converse with them respectfully, and encourage them in all humility. What I say now is what I have always said. This way of life is holy and good. Chastity is its adornment, discretion its renown. Organized by the Fathers and predestined by the Holy Spirit, it is eminently suited for the saving of souls. How could I possibly condemn or contemn an Order I praise so highly? I remember how, on occasion, I was welcomed as a guest in some monasteries of the Order. I pray that the Lord will reward his servants for the abundant kindness they lavished on me when I was ill, and for the honor they rendered me, which they themselves were more worthy than I to receive. I have asked them to pray for me.[17] I have attended their community meetings.[18] I have spoken a great deal with many of them about the Bible and the salvation of souls, both publicly in chapter, and privately.[19] I have never secretly or openly encouraged anyone to leave that Order and come to ours; in fact, I rebuffed many monks who wanted to come, and if any came knocking, I turned them

17. Apart from oral requests, Bernard ends two of his letters to Peter the Venerable by soliciting the prayers of "the holy brethren of Cluny" (*Letter* 228, 2; PL 398a; trans. James, no. 305, p. 376 and *Letter* 387; PL 591d; trans. James, no. 308, p. 379).

18. Community meetings, *collationes*, are described in J. Leclercq, *The Love of Learning and the Desire for God* (New York: Mentor, 1962), p. 169.

19. Lit. "privately, *in cameris*". The room labeled *camera* in Dr Conant's plan of Cluny (plate IV, in *Petrus Venerabilis, 1156–1956*) measures approx. 100′ × 30′. *Camera* is a generic term covering any sort of room; Bernard is probably referring to small rooms suitable for private consultation.

away.[20] Br Nicholas I sent back to the Abbey of St Nicholas,[21] and you will recall that I returned two of your own monks. Moreover, you know well enough that there were two abbots of the Order who wanted to change, and were even making plans to do so, and that it was only my advice to the contrary that deterred them from resigning. I won't mention any names since you know who they are, and that they are my own close friends.[22] Why should people think or say that I reject an order, when I advise my friends to remain in it, when I send back its monks if they come to us; and from it earnestly ask prayers for myself and accept them with gratitude?

III. 5. Perhaps the mere fact of my belonging to another order is sufficient to give rise to suspicions on this score. But if this is so, it must also be true that you are insulting us by not adopting our way of life. By the same token, we would have to take it for granted that celibates and married folk are at variance, simply because their lives are moderated by different Church laws, and that monks and regulars are always at odds due to differences in observances. We would never guess that Noah, Daniel, and Job share the same kingdom, since we know they followed very different paths of virtue.[23] Finally, we would have to affirm that either Mary or

20. Bernard's practice may be culled from several of his letters, e.g. nos 3, 32ff., 65ff., 253, 382, 396 (trans. James, nos. 3, 33f., 68ff., 328, 419, 428.) Cf. note 172.

21. The abbey of Saint Nicholas-aux-Bois, ruled at this time by Simon, said to be a brother of William of St Thierry, was situated in the diocese of Laon. Br Nicholas may be the monk to whom Bernard refers in one of his letters to Simon (*Letter* 84; PL 205f.; trans. James, no. 86, p. 124).

22. One of these abbots very probably was William himself. His attraction to the Cistercian life dated from his first meeting with Bernard in 1118 (Cf. *Vita Prima* II, cap. vii, no. 33; PL 185:246d). His application to join, made shortly before the composition of the *Apologia,* was rejected by Bernard. Cf. *Letter* 86, 2 (PL 210d; trans. James, no. 88, p. 128).

23. Basing himself on an interpretation of Ezek 14:14 f., Gregory the Great saw in Noah, Daniel and Job types of the different orders in the Church. Noah represented the church authorities, Daniel the religious, and Job the good lay-folk (*Moralia,* I, 20; *Sources chrétiennes,* 32 [Paris, 1952],p. 152). Bernard often employs the same categories: e.g. Sermon 35, *De diversis*

Martha or both failed to please the Lord, since their efforts to do this were so very unlike.[24]

If all this were correct, there would be neither peace nor harmony in the Church, arrayed as it is, like the queen in the Psalm,[25] with a wide variety of religious orders. If it is true that by entering one order, a man is bound to hold the other orders in contempt, or to believe that this is their attitude toward him, how can he possibly find peace and security in his vocation, since it is quite impossible for one man to join all the orders? At the same time, no one order is suitable for everybody.

I am not so dull that I cannot recognize Joseph's robe here. I don't mean the Joseph who freed Egypt from bodily famine, but the one who saved the world from death of soul and body. This robe was famous for its many colors; it was marked out by a glorious variety. The robe was dipped in blood, not goat's blood signifying sin, but lamb's blood, which typifies innocence. This means that it was his own blood, not someone else's. For he, surely, is the meek lamb that was speechless, not before shearers, but before slayers. He

---

(*S. Bernardi Opera*, VI, p. 200); *In Nativ.*, I, 7 (*ibid.*, IV, p. 249); *In Dom. Palm.*, I, 4 (*ibid.*, V, p. 45). The author of the *Nouvelle réponse* proposes a slightly different interpretation of the same three figures (ed. J. Leclercq, *Recueil d'études sur saint Bernard et ses écrits* [Rome: Edizioni di Storia e Letteratura, 1966], II, p. 83). Cf. G. Penco, "Temi ed aspetti ecclesiologici della tradizione monastica" in *Studia Monastica*, 10 (1968), p. 66; P. Deseille, "Théologie de la vie monastique selon S. Bernard" in *Théologie de la vie monastique* (Paris: Aubier, 1961), pp. 519–521.

24. Martha and Mary are the traditional types of the active and the contemplative way of life. For the first phases of the history of the theme, up to the time of Augustine, cf. Daniel Csanyí, "*Optima Pars*: die Auslegungsgeschichte von Lk 10, 36–42 bei den Kirchenvätern der ersten vier Jahrhunderte" in *Studia Monastica*, 2 (1960), pp. 5–78. Peter the Venerable considers the hard-working Cistercians to have chosen Martha's part (*Letters* I, 28; PL 129a). The author of the *Nouvelle réponse* follows him in this, as in other matters, l. 171f., *op. cit.*, p. 79. The same retort is put in the mouth of the Cluniac in the *Dialogus inter Cluniacensem Monachum et Cisterciensem de Diversis utriusque Ordinis Observantiis* (ed. Martène and Durand, *Thesaurus Novorum Anecdotorum*, V, col. 1569ff.). Cf. Knowles, *Cistercians and Cluniacs*, p. 32. Bernard himself refers to the idea in no. 12.

25. Cf. Ps 45:14.

D

committed no sin, and yet he took away the sins of the world. The text continues: "They sent to Jacob and said, 'We found this. See whether or not it is your son's robe.' "[26] You also Lord, see whether this is your beloved Son's robe. All-powerful Father, recognize the many-colored garment you have made for your Anointed. Some men you have set aside as apostles, others as prophets. Some are preachers of the Gospel, others are pastors or teachers or fulfill some other role in the wondrous decoration of this garment. All contribute to the perfection of the saints, and together all press on toward mature manhood, according to the measure of the age of Christ's fullness.[27] O God, take note also of the dark hue of his precious blood, sprinkled over the garment, the splendid and victorious sign of obedience. "Why," the text asks, "is your apparel all red?" He answers, "Because I have trodden the wine-press alone. From the peoples not a man was with me."[28]

6. So he became obedient to the Father, and came to the wine-press of the cross, which he trod alone. His own arm alone lent him support, according to what we read elsewhere: "I am alone until I pass."[29] Therefore O God, lift him up. Give him that name which is above all names, so that at the name of Jesus, every knee should bend in heaven, on earth, and under the earth.[30] "He has ascended on high and taken captives; he has given gifts to men."[31] What gifts are these? To his Bride, the Church, he left his own robe as a pledge of her inheritance, a many-colored robe, woven from top to bottom.[32] It is many-colored because of the many different orders that are distinguished within it; it is seamless because of the undivided unity of a love that cannot be torn apart,[33] as it is written: "Who will separate us from the love of Christ?"[34] First, hear how the robe is many-colored: "There are varieties of graces, but the same Spirit;

---

26. Gen 37:32.   27. Cf. Eph 4:11f.   28. Is 63:2f.
29. Ps 141:10.   30. Cf. Phil 2:9f.
31. Cf. Ps 68:18; Eph 4:8.   32. Jn 19:23.
33. Cf. *Letter* 334: "The tunic of Christ is the unity of the Church which does not admit of being torn or divided. What has thus been woven, what the Holy Spirit has thus unified, cannot be torn up by men" (PL 537d; trans. James, no. 246, p. 326; cf. *Letter* 219, 2; PL 384a; trans. James, no. 293, p. 360).
34. Rom 8:35.

there are different works, but the same Lord."[35] Then, after listing
the various charisms, which correspond to the different hues of
the many-colored robe, the Apostle adds the following, to show
that it is also seamless, woven from top to bottom: "All these are
the work of one and the same Spirit, who apportions to each as he
pleases.[36] For love has been poured forth in our hearts by the Holy
Spirit, who has been given to us."[37]

Therefore, let there be no division within the Church. Let it
remain whole and entire according to its inherited right. Concerning
the Church it has been written: "At your right hand stands the
queen in a golden robe, interlaced with variety."[38] This is why
different people receive different gifts. One man is allotted one kind,
one another, irrespective of whether he be a Cistercian or a Cluniac,
a regular or one of the laity. This applies to every order and to all
languages, to both sexes, to every age and condition of life, everywhere and always, from the first man down to the last. It is for this
reason that the robe is described as being ankle-length,[39] since it
reaches down to the furthest extremities. "Nothing," as the
Prophet says, "is concealed from its warmth."[40] In this way it fits
the wearer, since another part of the Bible says of him: "He reaches
mightily from one end to the other, he orders all things well."[41]

IV. 7. Therefore, let us all work together to form a single robe,
and let this one robe include us all. I say this because, although the
components are many and varied, my dove, my fair and perfect
one is one only.[42] It is not I by myself, nor you without me, nor a
third person on his own, who can form this one robe, but all of us
together, provided we take care to maintain the unity of the Spirit
in the bond of peace.[43] I repeat, it is not our Order alone, nor yours
alone that makes up this unity, but ours and yours together, unless,
of course, there be envy and mutual offense.[44] Then we would be

---

35. 1 Cor 12:4f.   36. 1 Cor 12:11.   37. Rom 5:5.   38. Ps 45:9.
39. Gen 37:23.   40. Ps 19:6.   41. Wis 8:1.
42. A combination of Song 2:10 and Song 6:8. The same composite text
appears in *De Consideratione*, II, viii, no. 5 (*S. Bern. Op.*, III, p. 423).
43. Cf. Eph 4:3.   44. Cf. Gal 5:26.

devouring each other, and both of us would be consumed,[45] and the Apostle could not unite us to the Husband to whom we have been betrothed; he could not present us as a pure bride to Christ.[46]

In the Song of Songs, the Bride says: "Set love in order about me,"[47] as if to say that though love is one, yet it can be set in order as if it were many. What am I saying? I am a Cistercian myself, but this does not mean that I reject Cluniacs. On the contrary, I am very fond of them; I praise and extol them. You might ask: "Why don't you join them if you think so highly of them?" My reply is this: because, as the Apostle says, "everyone should remain in the vocation in which he was called."[48] If you ask why, in that case, I didn't pick the Cluniacs in the beginning, I would answer that, as the Apostle says elsewhere, "all things are lawful, but not everything is to be recommended."[49] It is not that this Order is not holy and virtuous. The reason is that I am an unspiritual man, sold under sin.[50] I knew that my soul was so weak as to require a stronger remedy. Different remedies are prescribed for different illnesses; the more serious the illness, the more drastic the remedy. Take the case of two men with fever, one with quartan, the other with tertian. The man with the quartan fever might recommend to the other that he take only water, pears, and other cold dishes, whereas he himself has none of these things, but takes wine and hot dishes instead, such

---

45. Cf. Gal 5:15.   46. 2 Cor 11:2.

47. Cf. Song 2:4 (Vulg.): *Ordinavit in me caritatem.* Usually when Bernard speaks of the "ordering of love," *ordinatio caritatis,* he is referring to an alignment of man's affections with God's will, and the consequent exclusion of anything inordinate. It is a question of practical discretion in love, the ability to assess priorities realistically. Cf. Sermon 49, 6, *On the Song of Songs* (*S. Bern. Op.,* II, pp. 75 f., trans. Luddy, II, pp. 60 f.). In the present instance, however, the nuance is different. Noting the various forms of religious life, and perhaps punning on the word *order,* Bernard here touches on a point that he will be covering in no. 8. The unitive power of love does not suppress multiplicity, but integrates or orders it. For a general treatment of the *ordinatio caritatis,* cf. M. Standaert, "Le principe de l'ordination dans la théologie spirituelle de S. Bernard" in *Collectanea O.C.R.,* 8 (1946), pp. 176–216.

48. 1 Cor 7:20; cf. Bernard's *Letter* 32, 3 (PL 138b; trans. James, no. 33, p. 67).

49. 1 Cor 10:22.   50. Cf. Rom 7:14.

things being more suited to his condition. Who could cavil at this? If the second man were to ask: "Why don't you drink water yourself, if you think so highly of it?", wouldn't he be justified in replying: "It is for your benefit that I give it to you; it is for my own that I go without."?[51]

8. It may equally be asked why I don't join all orders, since I praise them all. For it is a fact that I do praise them all, and love any that live good and virtuous lives in the Church. I am attached to all the orders by love, but it is in one alone that I find my work. Yet I trust that my love will so bring it about that I will share also in the fruits of these orders to which I do not belong. I will go even further. You yourself will have to be very careful, for it could happen that your work be fruitless; on the other hand it is quite impossible that my love for your work be so. Oh, how bold is love! One man works without loving, a second man loves without working. The first man's labor is lost, the other man's love will never fail.

Why wonder at this variety during the time of exile, while the Church is on pilgrimage? Why wonder that its unity is also plurality? Probably even in the homeland, where unity will be supreme, there will be different forms of equality. Thus it is written: "In my Father's house there are many rooms."[52] Just as there are many rooms in a single house, so there are many different orders in the one Church. Just as on earth there are different graces, but the one spirit, so in heaven there are different types of glory within a single house. In both cases unity consists in the singleness of love. Here below diversity resides in the differences of orders and the various allotments of work; in heaven diversity will take the form

---

51. What Bernard seems to be saying is that it is better medicine to treat the cause of illness rather than its symptoms. In the example given, both men are intermittently feverish, but the difference in the cycles of their paroxysms indicates that different causes are operative, and hence that different remedies are required. Hippocrates regarded the quartan as the mildest of all fevers, since it often heralds the recession of more serious disorders (cf. *Of the Epidemics*, I, iii, 2; trans. F. Adams in *Great Books of the Western World*, No. 10 [Chicago: *Encyclopaedia Britannica*, 1952], p. 49).

52. Jn 14:2.

of an obvious and well-ordered gradation of merit. The Church understands this mingling of harmony and discord when it says: "He led me along paths of virtue for his name's sake."[53] Paths is plural, virtue singular, hence neither the diversity of works nor the unity of the workmen is overlooked.

The Church looks forward to this manifold unity, and devotedly sings glad tidings: "The squares of Jerusalem will be paved with pure gold, and all her streets will cry, 'Alleluia'."[54] The squares and the streets may be understood to represent the different crowns and glories. In the gold with which the whole of the city is said to be adorned, and in the single song of Alleluia, you may recognize how alike are the different types of glory, and understand how it is that many minds can be united in a single spirit of devotion.

9. There are many paths that can be taken, for the dwelling-places to which we journey are many. Whatever path a man is taking, let him not be so concerned about alternative routes that he lose sight of his destination.[55] Let him be sure that by following the path he is on, he will eventually arrive at one of the dwelling-places, and will not be left outside his Father's house.

"Star differs from star," says St Paul, "and so will it be at the resurrection of the dead."[56] All the saints will shine like the sun in their Father's kingdom, yet because of differences in merit, some will shine more than others. In the present age, of course, merits cannot be assessed, but in the next, men will be able to judge them easily enough. Here below we see only the works done, there we shall be able to penetrate to the heart, since the sun of Righteousness will reach out in all directions to disclose the hidden depths of hearts. At present, nothing is concealed from its warmth; then, nothing will

53. Ps 23:3.

54. Tob 13:22. Bernard quotes the same version of the text in Sermon 76, 5, *On the Song of Songs* (*S. Bern. Op.*, II, p. 257; trans. Luddy, II, p. 405). Dom Leclercq notes that no trace of this rendering can be found in any of the available Latin versions of Tobias, although the responsory *Plateae tuae* for the third week after Easter is very close to it (*Recueil*, I, p. 306).

55. Lit. "that he deviate from the one virtue." The reference is to the interpretation of Ps 23:3 given in the previous paragraph.

56. 1 Cor 15:41f.

be untouched by its splendor. Judgment passed on the basis of works alone is risky, since it is liable to error; it often happens that those who do the most work have the least virtue. [Here ends my defense.]

AGAINST DETRACTORS

V. 10. It has come to my notice that there are some members of our Order who are speaking unfavorably of other orders, contrary to what the Apostle says: "Do not pass judgment prematurely, before the coming of the Lord. He will light up things hidden in darkness, and disclose the designs of the heart."[57] Instead of submitting to God's justices, such people wish to set up their own.[58] This being the case, they belong neither to our Order, nor to any other. They may live orderly lives, but their haughty language makes them citizens of Babylon, which means "disorder";[59] they are sons of darkness and children of hell, where there is no order but unending chaos.[60]

To you brothers am I speaking, who scorn others and rely on your own virtues, even after hearing the Lord's parable of the Pharisee and the Publican. I have heard it said that you speak of yourselves as the only ones with any virtue, as holier than everyone else, and the only monks who live according to the Rule; as far as you are concerned, other monks are simply transgressors.

11. To begin with, who are you to pass judgment on another's servant? It is before their own master that they stand or fall.[61] Who made you their judges? It is a disorder if you are so proud of your own Order that you fret about the splinters in your brothers' eyes, without bothering to get rid of the log in your own. You glory in the Rule, yet you yourselves don't keep it. You pass judgment prematurely, contrary to the Gospel, and on the servants of another contrary to the Apostle. The Rule itself has to accord

---

57. 1 Cor 4:5.
58. Cf. Sermon 14, 1, *On the Song of Songs* (*S. Bern. Op.*, I, p. 76; trans. Luddy, I, p. 127).
59. Lit. "confusion." Cf. Sermon 5, 9, *In Dedic.* (*S. Bern. Op.*, V. p. 395).
60. Cf. Job 10:22.   61. Rom 14:4.

with both Gospel and Apostle, otherwise it would be no rule at all, since it would be itself untrue. Listen to this and learn right order, you who violate good order by saying disparaging things about other Orders: "You hypocrite! First remove the log from your own eye so that you will see clearly to take the splinter from your brother's."[62] Do you want to know to which log I am referring? It is the long, large log of pride,[63] which makes you think you are something, when in fact you are nothing.[64] You foolishly rejoice in your own soundness, and notwithstanding the log, you scoff at others because of their splinters. You say: "O God, I give you thanks that I am not like the rest of men, unjust, extortioners, and adulterers."[65] Don't stop now! Why not also include detractors? Detraction is just as much a splinter as the others; how is it that when you list the other splinters so meticulously you say nothing about this? If you think that it is a matter of little or no importance, listen to what the Apostle has to say about it. "Detractors," he says, "will not inherit God's kingdom."[66] God gives this threat in one of the Psalms; from the context we know that it applies to detractors. He says: "I will rebuke you and accuse you to your face."[67] The man who shifts his gaze from himself, and is more interested in others' faults than in his own, will be wrenched back and made to take stock of himself; and it will serve him right.[68]

VI. 12. They retort: "How can these monks be said to keep the Rule? They wear furs[69] and they eat meat[70] and fat.[71] Every day

62. Mt 7:5.

63. Cf. *The Steps of Humility*, IV, 14 (*S. Bern. Op.*, III, p. 27; trans. Webb and Walker, p. 35).

64. Cf. Gal 6:3.   65. Lk 18:11.   66. 1 Cor 6:10.   67. Ps 50:21.

68. Cf. *The Steps of Humility*, XI, 39 (*S. Bern. Op.*, III, p. 46; trans. Webb and Walker, p. 64).

69. Peter the Venerable pointed to the concession of furs as a sign of Cluny's solicitude toward the infirmity of its members (*Letters* IV, 17; PL 328f.). The authorities he adduces in favor of the practice in *Letters* I, 28 (PL 120c) are repeated by Bernard, *infra*, no. 12. However, when Peter came to write the *Statutes*, he restricted the use of furs, rejecting outright whatever appeared expensive or showy, and allowing only sheepskins and goatskins (*Statute* 17, PL 1030).

70. Further on, Bernard seems to indicate that meat was not, in fact, served

they have three or four different dishes, which the Rule forbids,[72] and they leave out the work it enjoins.[73] Many points of their Rule they modify or extend or restrict as they like." This is so; no one could deny it. But look at God's rule, with which St Bendict's regulations agree. It says that "the kingdom of God is within you,"[74] it does not consist in outward things like bodily clothing and food,

---

in the common refectory at Cluny. Two large fish courses took its place (no. 20), or alternatively, those who wanted meat transferred to the infirmary (no. 21). Peter the Venerable penned a scorching denunciation of meat-eating in the Cluniac dependencies (Introduction, p. 18, *supra*). He repeated his prohibition in *Statute* 12 (PL 1029c).

71. The first Cistercians rejected the use of fat as contrary to the Rule (*Ex. Parv.*, XV; PL 166:1507; trans. Larkin, *op. cit.*, p. 262. *Ex. Magn.* I, 20; ed. Griesser, p. 75, l. 25 f.). At the time the *Apologia* was written Cluny allowed fat every day of the year. In the *Statutes* Peter the Venerable prohibited its use on Friday (no. 10; PL 1028 cd), and during advent (no. 15; PL 1030b).

72. Ch. 39 of the Rule allows two cooked dishes at the principal meal, "so that those who cannot eat one, can make their meal on the other." Cîteaux adhered to this stipulation (*Ex. Parv.*, *loc. cit.*). Peter the Venerable argued that if two dishes were allowed because of individual infirmities, then it is all right to give three or four for the same reason (*Letters* I, 28, PL 126b), and the author of the *Riposte* added that a truly temperate man can eat any number of dishes without giving way to gluttony (*op. cit.*, l. 293, p. 317; l. 371, p. 319). The Cluniac in the *Dialogus* maintains that there are really only two dishes served; the extras which charity prompts are not counted (*op. cit.*, col. 1637).

73. Benedict envisages a monk giving about six hours a day to work. A return to manual work was one of the characteristic features of the Cistercian reform (cf. *Ex. Magn.* I, 20; ed. Griesser, p. 75, l. 33), made necessary, perhaps, by the poverty that surrounded the beginnings of the New Monastery. Initially Peter the Venerable had defended Cluny by saying that since work was merely a cure for idleness (Rule, ch. 48), it was not mandatory if monks could fill in their day with some other occupation (*Letters* I, 28; PL 128d). The same position is taken by the author of the *Nouvelle réponse*. Work is only a concession as far as monks are concerned (l. 235, p. 81), an antidote to their weakness in contemplation (l. 175, p. 79; cf. Rule, ch. 48). Later Peter the Venerable based his case on prudential reasons, e.g., work had to be omitted simply because there was no work available that monks could profitably and decently do (*Letters* IV, 17; PL 329d). In the *Statutes*, Peter makes a complete *volte-face*. Work must be found for everybody, he insists, otherwise monks will spend the day gossiping or just dozing in the sun (*Statute* 39, PL 1037a). That Bernard does not treat more amply of work's omission at Cluny may perhaps be ascribed to the *Apologia's* premature conclusion (no. 30). 74. Lk 17:21.

but in man's interior virtues. "The kingdom of God," as the
Apostle says, "is not food and drink, but righteousness and peace
and joy in the Holy Spirit."[75] And also: "The kingdom of God
consists in power, not in word."[76] You cast aspersions on the
Fathers because of mere outward observances, while you yourself
don't bother about the more important spiritual regulations laid
down by the Rule. You gulp down the camel and strain out the
gnat.[77] How absurd! Great care is taken to see that the body is
clothed according to the Rule, whilst the Rule is broken by leaving
the soul naked. A good deal of attention is given to getting a robe
and cowl for the body, since a man is not reckoned a monk without
them. Meanwhile there is no thought for his spiritual attire, the
spirit of prayer and humility.

There are people who go clad in tunics and have nothing to do
with furs who, nevertheless are lacking in humility. Surely
humility in furs is better than pride in tunics. After all, God himself
made clothes for the first man out of animal skins;[78] John the
Baptist in the desert wore a leather girdle round his waist;[79] and
Benedict himself, in his hermit days, wore animal skins instead of
a tunic.[80]

We fill our stomachs with beans and our minds with pride. We
condemn rich food as though it were not better to take delicate
fare in moderation than to bloat ourselves to belching-point with
vegetables.[81] Remember that Esau was censured because of lentils,
not meat,[82] Adam was condemned for eating fruit, not meat,[83] and

---

75. Rom 14:17.   76. 1 Cor 4:20.   77. Cf. Mt 23:24.
78. Cf. Gen 3:21.   79. Cf. Mt 3:4.

80. Lit. "the very one who made the regulations about tunics." Benedict's
career as a monk was formally initiated by his receiving from the hand of the
priest Romanus, the *melota*, a rough sheepskin garment adopted by most of
the Eastern monks. Later, when some shepherds spied Benedict moving
among the bushes in his *melota*, they thought him some strange sort of wild
animal. Cf. Gregory the Great, *Dialogues*, II, ch. 1; trans. Dom Justin McCann
(Rugby: Princethorpe Priory, 1941), pp. 12-13.

81. Cf. Sermon 30, *On the Song of Songs* (*S. Bern. Op.*, I, p. 217: trans.
Luddy, I, p. 362).

82. Cf. Gen 26:34.   83. Cf. Gen 3:17.

Jonathan was under sentence of death for tasting honey, not meat.[84] On the other hand, Elijah ate meat without coming to grief,[85] Abraham set a delicious meat-dish before the angels,[86] and God himself ordered sacrifices of the flesh of animals.[87]

Surely it is more satisfactory to take a little wine on account of weakness than to quaff down greedy draughts of water, since Paul counseled Timothy to take a little wine.[88] The Lord himself drank wine and was called a wine-bibber because of it.[89] He gave it to his Apostles to drink, and from it established the Sacrament of his Blood.[90] On the other hand, he would not countenance water-drinking at a marriage-feast,[91] and it was at the waters of Meribah that he punished the people severely for their complaining.[92] David too, was afraid to drink the water he desired,[93] and those of Gideon's men who, in their eagerness to drink from the stream, fell on their faces, were considered unworthy for the fight.[94]

What have you to boast about in your manual work? Martha worked as you do and was rebuked, whereas Mary remained still and was praised.[95] Paul says quite plainly that "bodily work is of some value, but spirituality is valuable in every way."[96] The best sort of work is that to which the Prophet refers when he says: "I am in labor because of my grief,"[97] and, "I think of God and I am ravished, and I exert myself."[98] To prevent us thinking that he is speaking of bodily exertion he adds: "And my spirit grows weary."[99] It is spiritual work to which he is referring, since it is the spirit and not the body that is wearied by it.

VII. 13. You may object: "It looks as though you are so concerned with the spiritual side of things that you discredit even those material observances imposed on us by the Rule." No, such things ought to be done, but without neglecting the others.[100] At the

---

84. Cf. 1 Sam 14:29.   85. Cf. 1 Kings 17:6.   86. Cf. Gen 18:8.
87. Cf. Ex 20:24.   88. Cf. 1 Tim 5:23   89. Cf. Mt. 11:19.
90. Cf. Mt 26:27.   91. Cf. Jn 2:1f.   92. Cf. Num 20:6.
93. Cf. 2 Sam 23:16.   94. Cf. Jud 7:5.
95. Cf. Lk 10: 36f. See note 24 *supra*, p. 39.   96. 1 Tim 4:18.
97. Ps 6:6.   98. Ps 77:6.   99. *Ibid.*
100. Cf. Mt 23:23.

same time, if it happen that one or other element must be left aside, it is better that it be the material. For, just as the soul is more important than the body, so spiritual practices are more fruitful than material ones. But as for you, if you have become so complacent about your bodily observances that you look down on those who cannot follow suit, then it is you who are the real transgressor. You lose your grip on more important things and cling to trifles, whereas Paul tells us to "seek the better gifts."[101] In this matter of disparaging your brothers, humility is lost when you put yourself on a pedestal, and charity when you trample on others, and surely these are the great gifts. You do well when you wear yourself out with all manner of hard work. You do well when, by the austerity of the Rule, you put to death whatever is earthly in you.[102] At the same time it could happen that the man you judge so unfavorably because he has only a little of what is of limited value, i.e. bodily work, may be richer than you in what is of value in every way, i.e. spirituality.[103] Who, may I ask, keeps the Rule better? Surely it is he who is himself better. And who is better, the humble man or the weary man? Surely it is he who has learned from the Lord to be gentle and humble of heart. This is the one who, like Mary, has chosen the better part; and it shall not be taken away from him.[104]

14. If you think that all those who make profession of the Rule are obliged to keep it literally without any possibility of dispensation,[105] then I dare say, you yourself fail as much as the Cluniac.[106] It may be that he is deficient in many points of external observance, but even you can't avoid an occasional fault, and you know, of course, that anyone who fails in a single point is guilty of everything.[107] If, on the other hand, you admit that some things can be changed by dispensation, then it must be true that both you and the

---

101. 1 Cor 12:31.
103. Cf. 1 Tim 4:8.

102. Cf. Col 3:5.
104. Cf. Lk 10:42.

105. Bernard's own mind on this subject is exposed at length in *Monastic Obligations and Abbatial Authority* (*infra*). See also *De Consideratione*, III, iv, 18 (*S. Bern. Op.*, III, p. 445).
106. "The Cluniac." lit. "he."
107. Jas 2:10: "If a man keep the entire law, but fail in a single point, he is guilty of everything."

Cluniac are keeping the Rule, though each in his own way. You keep it more strictly; he, perhaps, keeps it more reasonably.

I don't mean by this that external means can be overlooked, or that the man who does not employ them will quickly become spiritual. Spiritual things are certainly higher, but there is little hope of attaining them or of receiving them without making use of external exercises, as it is written: "It is not the spiritual that comes first but the physical; and then comes the spiritual."[108] Jacob was unfit to win Rachel's longed-for embraces until he had knowledge of Lia.[109] So too we read in one of the Psalms: "strike up a song, and play on the drum."[110] This means, "Take up spiritual things but first make use of physical things." The man in the best position is he who makes use of both as occasion demands, and with discernment.

15. If this is going to be a letter, it is time it came to an end.[111] I have taken up the pen, Father, as you asked, and rebuked those of our monks who have been speaking unfavorably of your Order, and I have, at the same time cleared myself of unfounded suspicion on this count. However, there is something more I must say. Because I have been unsparing with our own monks, it may appear as though I am condoning a number of elements in your Order, which are not to your liking, I know, and which are, in fact, avoided by all good monks. Though such abuses are in the Order, I hope they are not of the Order.[112] No order can have room for disorder, and whatever is disorderly cannot belong to an Order. Hence my objections must be regarded as helping to promote the

108. 1 Cor 15:46. Bernard often quotes this text. Cf. E. Gilson, *The Mystical Theology of St. Bernard* (London: Sheed and Ward, 1955), pp. 37f.

109. Cf. Gen 29:23.

110. Ps 81:2.

111. A lost Marmoutier manuscript mentioned by Mabillon, and dating perhaps from the twelfth century, describes the *Apologia* as made up of two letters, presumably with the break at the end of this paragraph. Cf. Introduction to the critical edition of the *Apologia* in *S. Bern. Op.*, III, p. 67; Leclercq, *Recueil*, I, p. 244; II, pp. 123f.; W. Williams, *St Bernard of Clairvaux* (Manchester University Press, 1953), p. 348.

112. The distinction may be modeled on the Johannine "in the world" but not "of the world"; cf. Jn 17:15f.

Order, rather than as pulling it down. It is not for belonging to the Order that I rebuke men, but for their vices. So it is that I have no fear that those who really love the Order will be upset by what I am going to say. Quite the contrary, they will probably be grateful that I condemn the things which they themselves detest. If anyone is angry with me, this only proves that he has no real love for the Order, since he will not condemn the vices that are ruining it. To him I reply, in the words of St Gregory, that "it is better for scandal to arise than for truth to be abandoned."[113]

[The end of the section "Against Detractors."]

AGAINST EXCESSES

VIII. 16. It is said correctly that it was by holy Fathers that this way of life was organized;[114] they did not abrogate the Rule, they merely moderated its severity on account of the weak, so that more men might be saved. At the same time, I would hate to think that these holy Fathers would have commanded or allowed the many foolish excesses I have noticed in several monasteries. I am astonished that monks could be so lacking in moderation in matters of food and drink, and with respect to clothing and bedding, carriages and buildings. Things have come to such a pass that right order and religion are thought to be promoted, the more concern and pleasure and enthusiasm there is regarding such things. Abstemiousness is

---

113. Gregory the Great, *In Ezek.* I, vii, 5 (PL 76:842). The same text is quoted in Bernard's *Letter* 34, 2 (PL 140c), and *Letter* 78, 10 (PL 197a). The rubric following was not included in the primitive edition of the *Apologia*; cf. Introduction, *supra*, p. 9.

114. The sanctity of the founders was alleged as a justification of the Cluniac way of life. "If the Order of Cluny were not pleasing to God, then these holy Fathers would hardly have attained heavenly glory" (Letter of Peter of St John to Hato of Troyes in *Petrus Venerabilis, 1156-1956*, p. 50, l. 37). By summoning these very founders as witnesses for the prosecution (no. 23), Bernard shows that he is not attacking the Cluniac ideal, which is "good and holy" (no. 4), but the abuses which prevent its realization, and which Peter the Venerable himself would later try to suppress. "It is not for belonging to the Order that I rebuke men, but for their vices" (no. 15).

accounted miserliness, sobriety strictness, silence gloom. On the other hand, laxity is labeled discretion, extravagance generosity, talkativeness sociability, and laughter joy. Fine clothes and costly caparisons are regarded as mere respectability, and being fussy about bedding is hygiene. When we lavish these things on one another, we call it love.[115] Such love undermines true love. Such discretion disgraces real discretion. This sort of kindness is full of cruelty, for it so looks after the body that the soul is strangled. How can love pamper the flesh and neglect the spirit? What sort of discretion is it to give everything to the body and nothing to the soul? Is it kindness to entertain the maid and murder the mistress?[116] For this kind of mercy let no one hope to receive the mercy the Gospel promises through the mouth of Truth, to those who show mercy: "Blessed are the merciful, for they shall receive mercy."[117] Rather, he can expect that penalty called down by holy Job on those who are cruelly kind. Speaking in prophecy, rather than merely giving vent to his feelings, he said: "May he go unremembered; let him come to grief like a sterile tree." He then shows how such a punishment was deserved by adding: "He feeds the barren childless woman, and does no good to the widow."[118]

17. It is obvious, then, that the kindness of the flesh is inordinate and unreasonable. The flesh is barren and childless, and in the Lord's words "profits nothing."[119] Also, as the Apostle says, "it will not inherit God's kingdom."[120] Such kindness is ever on the alert to fulfill every whim, caring nothing for the sage's sound advice about looking after the soul. "Have mercy on your own soul," he says, "and you will please God."[121] It is a good thing to be

---

115. A similar list of misnomers is found in *Letter* 1, 4; (PL 75a; trans. James, p. 4).

116. The following section, down to the beginning of no. 18, is not found in the first edition of the text; cf. Introduction, p. 9.

117. Mt 5:7; cf. Bernard's *Letter* 1, 4 (PL 75b; trans. James, p. 4). The text seems to have been quoted fairly liberally by the Cluniacs.

118. Job 24:20f. The same text is quoted in a similar context in Sermon 35, 3, *On the Song of Songs* (S. Bern. Op., I, p. 250; trans. Luddy, I, p. 418).

119. Jn 6:63.   120. 1 Cor 15:50.

121. Eccles 30:24. A favorite text of St Bernard.

merciful to your own soul; it cannot fail to win that mercy which makes you pleasing to God. Any other sort of mercy is cruelty; it is not love but malevolence; it is not discretion but disorder. It feeds the barren childless women, (i.e. it follows the futile fancies of the flesh), while it does no good to the widow (i.e. it does nothing to cultivate the soul's virtues). The soul is indeed bereaved of its heavenly Bridegroom in this life, yet it has from the Holy Spirit the power to conceive and bring forth immortal children. These will, one day, enjoy their heavenly and incorruptible inheritance, provided they are reared by a guardian who is painstaking and devoted.

18. Nowadays, slackness has become so general that it is accepted as the normal thing. It is condoned by almost everyone unquestioningly and in all innocence, though not for the same reasons.[122] Some monks are detached in their use of such things, and so they incur little or no guilt. In other cases simplicity or charity or necessity is the motivation. There are monks who simply do what they are told, and who are quite prepared to act otherwise if they are so bidden. Some monks strive to avoid trouble with those among whom they live. They do not aim at fulfilling their own whims, but at safeguarding the peace of others. Finally there are monks who cannot withstand the majority voice which vigorously insists that such things are all right, and with all its might resists any attempt on the part of right reason to restrict or change anything.

IX. 19. Long ago, when the monastic Order began, who would have dreamed that monks could become so slack? Oh, how far away we have moved from Anthony and his contemporaries![123]

122. Cf. *Letter* 7, 19 (PL 104d; trans. James, no. 8, pp. 37f.).

123. Appeal to the authority of pre-Benedictine monastic tradition was quite usual in early Cistercian apologetics. Cf. *Ex. Magn.* I, 3f.; (ed. Griesser, pp. 50f.); William of St Thierry, *Vita Prima*, I, vii, 34 (PL 185: 247c); Aelred, *Speculum Caritatis*, II, 24 (PL 195:572c). See also L. Bouyer, *The Cistercian Heritage*, pp. 6f, and the letters of Edmund Bishop published under the title "Cluniacs and Cistercians" in *The Downside Review*, 52 (1934), pp. 223–230. The tendency to go beyond the letter of *St Benedict's Rule* indicates perhaps that the primary concern of the first Cistercians was for an integral monastic life rather than the material fulfillment of the regulations of the *Rule*.

If, from time to time, one of them paid a call on another, they were both so avid to receive spiritual nourishment from each other that they forgot all about their meals. Often they spent the whole day with fasting stomachs, but their minds were feasted. This is the correct order of precedence, when the greater in dignity is served first. This is real discretion, when the more important part is more amply provided for. Finally, this is true love, to tend carefully the souls for love of whom Christ died.

As for us, when we come together, to use the Apostle's words, it is not to eat the Lord's supper.[124] Nobody asks for the heavenly bread, and no one distributes it. There is nothing about the Bible or the salvation of souls. Jokes and laughter and chatter are all we hear. At table, while the mouth is filled with food the ears are nourished with gossip so absorbing that all moderation in eating is forgotten.

On meals

20. Meanwhile course after course is brought in.[125] Only meat is lacking, and to compensate for this two huge servings of fish are given. You might have thought that the first was sufficient, but even the recollection of it vanishes once you have set to on the second. The cooks prepare everything with such skill and cunning that the four or five courses already consumed are no hindrance to what is to follow, and the appetite is not checked by satiety. Once the palate is attracted to piquant flavors, ordinary things begin to pall; but if there is question of unusual flavors, desire is as quickly aroused as if the meal had not yet begun. The selection of dishes is so exciting that the stomach does not realize that it is being overtaxed. We turn up our noses at food that is unadulterated, as nature made it, and prefer to mix things together. We set aside their natural, God-given qualities so as to entice excess with hybrid

124. I Cor 11:20.
125. For the literary genre of this passage, cf. Introduction, p. 17. See also Leclercq, *The Love of Learning*, pp. 137f.

B

delicacies. Hunger, of course, has long since subsided; but there is always room for pleasure.

To take a single example: who could describe all the ways in which eggs are tampered with and tortured, or the care that goes into turning them one way and then turning them back? They might be cooked soft, hard, or scrambled. They might be fried or roasted, and occasionally they are stuffed. Sometimes they are served with other foods, and sometimes on their own. What reason can there be for all this variation except the gratification of a jaded appetite? A good deal of care is given to the appearance of a dish, so that the sense of sight is as much delighted by it as the palate. In this way, even when the stomach rumbles its repletion, the eyes can still feast on novelties. The eyes delight in colors, the palate in tastes, but the poor stomach can't see colors, and isn't tickled by tastes. It has to carry everything, and ends up being more oppressed than refreshed.

On drink

21. How can I recommend water-drinking, when we won't countenance adding water to the wine? All of us, because we are monks, seem to have stomach troubles, and so we have to follow the Apostle's advice and take some wine. I don't know why it is that we overlook the fact that it is a *"little* wine" that he recommends.[126] Even so, I only wish we could be content with plain wine, even though it be undiluted. It is embarrassing to speak of these things,[127] but it should be more embarrassing still to do them. If you are ashamed to hear them mentioned, you needn't be too ashamed to amend. The fact is that three or four times during a

---

126. 1 Tim 5:23. Cf. Sermon 30, 9, *On the Song of Songs* (*S. Bern. Op.* I, p. 218; trans. Luddy, I, p. 363). According to William of St Thierry, Bernard himself, partly because of his digestive ailment, took wine only rarely, and then well diluted: *Vita Prima*, I, viii, 39 (PL 185:250a).

127. In the primitive edition this sentence reads: "It is embarrassing to speak of such things that, had I not seen them with my own eyes, I would scarcely have credited. . . ."

meal, you might see a cup brought in, half-full, so that the different wines[128] can be sampled, more by aroma than by taste. It is not swallowed, but only caressed, since a seasoned palate can quickly distinguish one wine from another, and select the stronger. It is even alleged to be the custom in some monasteries to give the community honeyed or spiced wine on the major feasts.[129] Is this also on account of stomach troubles? As far as I can see all this is so designed to make drink as plentiful and pleasurable as possible. When the monk gets up from table and the swollen veins in his temple begin to throb, all he is fit for is to go back to bed. After all, if you force a man to come to the Office of Vigils before his digestion is complete,[130] all you will extract from him is a groan instead of a tone. So, when I get to bed I bewail my indisposition, not because I have sinned through gluttony, but because I have no room for more.

On those who stay in the infirmary without being ill

22. A funny story,[131] if it be true, told me by several people who can vouch for it, should, I think be mentioned here. They allege that there are hale and hearty young monks who abandon the common life, even though there is nothing wrong with them, and transfer to the infirmary. The Rule wisely allows the use of meat to the sick and to the very weak for the restoration of their strength,[132]

128. The primitive edition reads: " . . . so that the different wines can be sampled and tested, and the best among them selected. It is even alleged . . ."

129. Bernard had already attacked the use of spices and mulse at Cluny in his letter to Robert of Chatillion; *Letter* 1, 11 (PL 77b; trans. James, p. 8). Peter the Venerable condemned the practice in *Statute* 11 (PL 1028). The author of the *Riposte* staunchly defends the principle of giving something special on feast days, saying that it is only human, *humanum est* (l. 590, *op. cit.*, p. 324). St Bernard's attitude is sketched out more fully in Sermon 3, 2, *On Advent* (*S. Bern. Op.* IV, pp. 176 f.; trans. Luddy, *Principal Festivals*, I, p. 24).

130. Cf. *Rule of St Benedict* (hereafter RB), 8:2.

131. In the critical edition no. 22 begins with the last sentence of the preceding paragraph. This whole section, down to the mention of Macarius in no. 23, was added only in the second edition. Cf. Introduction, p. 25.

132. Cf. RB 36 and 39:11.

but these men desire it, not for the recuperation of an ailing body, but for the satisfaction of the whims of unbridled flesh.

I ask you,[133] is it a safe plan, while the enemy attacks and spears and arrows are flying round on all sides, is it a safe plan to act as though the war were ended and the foe defeated, to put down weapons and go off for a leisurely lunch, and then to lie down unarmed for a nap? What cowardice this is, my brave warriors! Your comrades are out wallowing in blood and gore, and here you are enjoying fine food and taking your morning sleep![134] Not for you to spend night and day making the most of your time in these evil days![135] You prefer to spend the long nights fast asleep, while the days you pass in idle chatter.[136] You are like those who cry "Peace" when there is no peace.[137] How is it that the Apostle's fierce reproach leaves you unashamed? He says: "You have not yet resisted to the point of shedding your blood."[138] Why do you not bestir yourself when you hear the terrible thunder of his threat? "If people say, 'There is peace and quiet,' a sudden catastrophe will strike them, as labor comes upon a woman with child, and no escape will be possible."[139]

How subtle is such medicine! It applies the bandage before any wound is inflicted, and it bemoans the limb as yet unsmitten. It massages the spot before it is bruised, and applies soothing ointment where there is no pain, and plaster where there is no abrasion.

23. To distinguish between invalids and those who are well, the sick are bidden to carry a walking-stick in their hands. This is an obvious necessity, for the stick has to support the pretense of illness where there is no sign of pallor or emaciation. Should we laugh or cry at such foolishness? Is this the way Macarius lived? Is it Basil's teaching or Anthony's command? Did the Fathers in Egypt adopt

133. This passage repeats many of the phrases Bernard used in his letter to Robert. *Letter* 1, 13 (PL 79a; trans. James, p. 9).

134. The author of the *Riposte* interprets this phrase as referring to the practice of going back to bed after the Office of Vigils: l. 974f.; *op. cit.*, p. 334.

135. Eph 5:16.

136. Cf. Peter the Venerable's *Statute* 29 (PL 1037a). See note 73.

137. Ezek 13:10.   138. Heb 12:4.   139. 1 Thess 5:3.

such a manner of life?[140] Finally, did those holy men whom they claim as the founders and teachers of their Order, Odo, Majolus, Odilo and Hugh, did they hold with such things or value them?[141] All these men were saints, and because of this they were in accord with what the Apostle said: "So long as we have food and clothing, we are content."[142] As for us, we are content only if we have all the food we can take, and clothing that is becoming.

On expensive and extravagant clothing

X. 24. Nowadays monks look for clothes that are stylish and will make a good impression rather than for something serviceable to keep out the cold. They don't opt for what is cheap, as the Rule recommends,[143] but for clothes that are of good quality and which look well. Poor miserable monk that I am, why have I lived to see us come to this? The monastic Order was the first order in the Church, it was out of it that the Church developed.[144] In all the earth there was nothing more like the angelic orders, nothing closer to the heavenly Jerusalem, our mother,[145] because of the beauty of its chastity and the fervor of its love. The Apostles were its moderators, and its members were those whom Paul often calls "the saints." It

140. Cf. note 123.

141. Odo († 942), Majolus (†994), Odilo (†1048) and Hugh (†1109), respectively the second, fourth, fifth and sixth abbots of Cluny, were considered the chief agents in the development of the Cluniac tradition. See note 114.

142. 1 Tim 6:8.

143. RB 55:7.

144. It was common practice in the Middle Ages to speak of organized monastic life as a continuation of the apostolic community described in Acts. Cf. H. de Lubac, *Exégèse Médiévale* (Paris: Aubier, coll. "Théologie," no. 42; 1959–1961), II, pp. 579f. See also *Ex. Magn.* I, 2 (ed. Griesser, pp. 49f.) and William of St Thierry, *Vita Prima*, I, iii, 15 (PL 185:235d). The idea is very ancient; Cassian knew two versions of it, the Alexandrian (cf. *Inst.* 11, 5 [S.C., no. 109, p. 65]) and the Jerusalem (cf. *Conf.* 18, 5 [S.C. no. 69, p. 14f.]). Cf. A. de Vogüé, "Monasticism and the Church in Cassian" in *Monastic Studies*, no. 3, pp. 19–52. Also G. M. Columbas, "The Ancient Concept of Monastic Life," *ibid.*, no. 4, p. 107.

145. Cf. Leclercq, *The Love of Learning*, pp. 59f.

was their practice to keep nothing as private property, for, as it is written, "distribution was made to each as he had need."[146] There was no scope for childish behavior. All received only as they had need, so that nothing was useless, much less novel or exotic. The text says, "as he had need;" this means, with regard to clothing, something to cover nakedness and keep out the cold.[147] Do you think they wore silks and satins,[148] and rode on mules worth two hundred gold pieces? Do you think their beds had catskin coverlets[149] and many-colored quilts,[150] if distribution was made only as any had need? I don't imagine they would have cared much about the value and color of their clothes. I don't think they would have bothered

146. Acts 4:35.

147. Although there is no manifest verbal dependence, the thought here approaches that of the corresponding sections of Cassian's *Institutes*. "A monk's clothing should simply cover his body, and avoid alike the shame of being naked and danger from the cold. It should not foster the growth of pride and vanity. . . ." (I, i, 2; S.C., no. 109, p. 38).

148. Lit. *galabrunum aut isembrunum*. The following elucidation by Prof. M. M. Postan is appended to David Knowles' article in *Petrus Venerabilis 1156-1956*. It is reproduced here and in note 150 by courtesy of the editors of the volume.

"*Galabruni:* almost certainly means yellowish brown cloth. *Gialla, gallo,* in the sense of yellow is used throughout the dyeing tariffs in pp. 506–507 of A. Doren's *Die florentiner Wollentuchindustrie*. That various colors could combine with brown to give it a tint is shown by the *tinctura de verdebruni* (*ibid.*, p. 519).

Isembruni: This is the most difficult of all, but the balance of probability is that 'isem' is a corruption of a very common Greek name for a thin silk fabric most commonly used for ecclesiastical vestments; *examiton* or *examitum* in Latin. In 1210 the Bishop of Poitiers promised the Abbey of Cluny an annual gift of *examitum* (*Bibl. de l'Ecole des chartes*, 2ᵉ serie, V, pp. 308 sqq.), cited in W. Heyd, *Histoire du commerce du Levant*, p. 699. In that case *isembrun* would be brown *examitum*."

Both of these fabrics were prohibited by Peter the Venerable in the *Statutes*, on the grounds that they were too showy for monks (no. 16; PL 1030c).

149. Catskins were forbidden by Peter the Venerable in *Statute* 17 (PL 1030d). He is especially wrathful toward the custom of importing them (col. 1031a).

150. Lit. *discolor barricanus*. To quote Prof. Postan once again: "*Barricani:* is almost certainly a corruption of *barrochino*, which is a form of *baldochino*, a cloth of levantine origin of silk and brocade: Doren, p. 519, and Heyd p. 697."

much about them at all. They were far too busy with their efforts to live in harmony, attached to one another and advancing in virtue. So it is said that "the company of believers was of one heart and one soul."[151]

25. Where is this zeal for unity nowadays? We give ourselves over to outward things, and abandon the true and lasting values of God's kingdom, which is within us.[152] Instead we go abroad, seeking some cold comfort from false and empty baubles. Not only has our religious life lost its inner vitality, we haven't even kept up an outward semblance. Look at the habit. It used to betoken humility. Nowadays, I am sorry to say, monks wear it as a sign of pride—so much so that it is difficult to get suitable material locally.[153] A single roll of cloth yields both monk's cowl and soldier's cloak. No one living in the world, no matter how high his position, even though he were a king or an emperor, would mind wearing our clothes, if they were only cut to fashion.

26. "Religion is in the heart," you say, "not in the habit."[154] I agree. How is it then, that when you want to buy a cowl, you have to make the rounds of all the cities, going through every center of commerce, inspecting markets and scrutinizing shops? Everywhere the whole stock must be brought out. You unroll huge bolts of cloth, finger them, examine them, hold them up to the daylight. You reject anything that is coarse or faded, but once something fine and bright takes your fancy, no matter what it costs, you won't rest until it is yours. May I ask whether this sort of thing comes from the heart, or do you do it without thinking? Is it intentionally that you contravene the Rule by seeking out very carefully what is unusual, and therefore more expensive, rather than something cheap? Any vice that shows up on the surface must have its source in the heart. A frivolous heart is known by frivolous conduct, external extravagance points to inward impoverishment, and soft

151. Acts 4:32.   152. Lk 17:21.   153. Cf. note 149.
154. The author of the *Riposte* actually does cite this maxim (l. 1313, *op. cit.*, p. 343), but since we do not possess his reply to this passage of the *Apologia* we do not know how he reacted to Bernard's remarks. Cf. *De Consideratione*, III, v, 20 (*S. Bern. Op.*, III, p. 447).

clothes are a sign of a soul without firmness. The fact is that there would not be so much concern for the body, if the fostering of spiritual values had not long since been neglected.

On the negligence of superiors

XI.   27. The Rule states that the superior will be responsible for the wrong-doing of his subjects,[155] and the Lord threatens through the Prophet that he will hold pastors to account for the blood of those who die in their sins.[156] This is why I am astonished that our abbots leave such things uncorrected. Perhaps, if I may say so, the reason is that they are hesitant about blaming others for the things they also do. After all, it is only human not to mind others taking the same liberties one allows oneself. This is what I say; I may be speaking brashly, but it is the truth. Oh, how has the light of the world become darkened, and the salt of the earth insipid?[157] Those whose lives should trace out a path of life for others, give instead, by their behavior, an example of pride. Those who are to lead the blind, have themselves been blinded.[158]

On riding in state

To take a single example: what evidence of humility does it give to go about in such pomp and circumstance, attended by so many retainers that an abbot's suite would be enough for two bishops? If I am not mistaken, I have seen anl abbot with sixty horse and more in his retinue. If you saw him ride by you would think he were the Lord of the Manor, or a provincial governor, instead of a monastic father and shepherd of souls. Orders are given for table-cloths and cups and dishes and candle-sticks to be loaded up. Packs are stuffed full, not so much with bedding as with decorative

155. Cf. RB 36:10.   156. Cf. Ezek 5:18.
157. Cf. Mt 5:13f.   158. Cf. Mt 15:14.

coverlets. A man can't go a dozen miles from home without carting all his chattels with him, as if he were going to the wars, or through a desert where the necessities of life are unobtainable. Is it too much to ask that you wash your hands from the same vessel that holds your wine? Do you think that a candle won't burn unless it be mounted on your own silver or gold candle-stick? Will you be sleepless without a parti-colored mattress and an imported coverlet? Wouldn't it be possible for the same servant to act as groom, waiter, and valet? Finally, if we are not able to make do without such a throng of men and beasts, couldn't we at least carry our own supplies with us, so that we don't become a burden on our hosts?[159]

On gold and silver images in monasteries

XII. 28. These are only small things; I am coming to things of greater moment. I merely mention these minor details because they happen to be rather common. I shall say nothing about the soaring heights and extravagant lengths and unnecessary widths of the churches, nothing about their expensive decorations and their novel images, which catch the attention of those who go in to pray, and dry up their devotion.[160] To me they seem like something out of

159. Peter the Venerable restricted a monk's retinue to three (*Statute* 40; PL 1037b). Prof. Knowles thinks that a couple of grooms and valets must be counted in addition ("The Reforming Decrees of Peter the Venerable" in *Petrus Venerabilis, 1156–1956* [Rome: Studia Anselmians, 1956], p. 15). It has been suggested that Bernard is thinking of Suger, the abbot of St Denis, to whom he later wrote: "As for myself, the whole and only thing that upset me was the pomp and splendor with which you traveled. This seemed to savor of arrogance" (*Letter* 78, 3; PL 193a; trans. James, no. 80, p. 112). This is possible, but we have no reason to believe that a taste for the splendid was an uncommon ecclesiastical failing at the time the *Apologia* was written.

160. This example of *praeteritio* is discussed in the Introduction, p. 13. Bernard's contemporaries would have instinctively applied Bernard's remarks to the huge church at Cluny, the largest in Christendom until the building of St Peter's. The building was some 600 feet long, with a width of about 130 feet, divided into five aisles. Its clerestory rose to about 100 feet. During the years immediately following the divulgation of the *Apologia*, from 1125–1130, Peter the Venerable, apparently uninhibited by its strictures, repaired

the Old Testament; but let them be, since it is all to the glory of God. However, as one monk to another, may I ask the question which a heathen poet put to his fellows. "Tell me, O priests," he said, "why is there gold in the holy place?"[161] I shall put the question slightly differently, I am more interested in the sense of the text than in its precise words. "Tell me, O poor men," this is my question, "tell me, O poor men—if you are really poor men—why is there gold in the holy place?" It is not the same for monks and bishops. Bishops have a duty toward both wise and foolish. They have to make use of material ornamentation to rouse devotion in a carnal people, incapable of spiritual things. But we no longer belong to such people. For the sake of Christ we have abandoned all the world holds valuable and attractive. All that is beautiful in sight and sound and scent we have left behind, all that is pleasant to taste and touch. To win Christ we have reckoned bodily enjoyments as dung.[162] Therefore, I ask you, can it be our own devotion we are trying to excite with such display, or is the purpose of it to win the admiration of fools and the offerings of simple folk? Living among gentiles, as we do, it seems that we now follow their example, and do service to their idols.[163]

---

and rebuilt on a grand scale. Cf. Kenneth J. Conant, "Cluniac Building during the Abbacy of Peter the Venerable" in *Petrus Venerabilis, 1156–1956*, pp. 121–127. St Bernard's own ideas on monastic architecture are incarnated in the abbey of Fontenay, Clairvaux's second daughter house, founded in 1118. The church was consecrated in 1147 by Pope Eugene III, and is virtually intact today. There is a series of views of the church, together with some of its history in *L'art cistercien* (Cahiers de la Pierre-qui-Vire, 1962, pp. 66–74, plates 1–14). An older and fuller treatment is Lucien Begule's *L'Abbaye de Fontenay et l'architecture cistercienne* (Lyons: Rey, 1912). Although the church is quite large (approx. 220′ × 60′ × 55′), it is quite unpretentious in design and very plain in furnishing. But as Abbot Cabrol remarks ("Cluny et Cîteaux" in *S. Bernard et son temps*, p. 27), the time would come when the Cistercians would erect churches far more flamboyant and expensive than anything Cluny produced. A glance at some of the examples of Baroque in L. Lekai's *White Monks* is instructive in this respect.

161. Perseus, *Satires*, II, 69 (*A Persi Flacci et D. Iuni Iuvenalis Saturae*, ed. W. V. Clausen [O.U.P., 1959], p. 11). Cf. Bernard's *De Moribus et Officio Episcoporum*, II, 5; PL 815d. See also Leclercq, *Love of Learning*, pp. 144f.

162. Phil 3:8.   163. Cf. Ps 106:35f.

Let me speak plainly. Cupidity, which is a form of idolatry,[164] is the cause of all this. It is for no useful purpose that we do it, but to attract gifts. You want to know how? Listen to the marvels of it all. It is possible to spend money in such a way that it increases; it is an investment which grows, and pouring it out only brings in more. The very sight of such sumptuous and exquisite baubles is sufficient to inspire men to make offerings, though not to say their prayers. In this way, riches attract riches, and money produces more money. For some unknown reason, the richer a place appears, the more freely do offerings pour in. Gold-cased relics catch the gaze and open the purses. If you show someone a beautiful picture of a saint, he comes to the conclusion that the saint is as holy as the picture is brightly colored. When people rush up to kiss them, they are asked to donate. Beauty they admire, but they do no reverence to holiness. This is the reason that churches are decked out, not merely with a jewelled crown, but with a huge jewelled wheel, where circles of lamps compete in radiance with precious stones.[165] Instead of candle-sticks we see tree-like structures, made of much metal and with exquisite workmanship, where candles and gems sparkle equally.[166] Do you think such appurtenances are meant to stir penitents to compunction, or rather to make sight-seers agog? Oh, vanity of vanities, whose vanity is rivalled only by its insanity![167] The walls of the church are aglow, but the poor of the Church go hungry. The stones of the church are covered with gold, while its children are left naked. The food of the poor is taken to feed the

164. Cf. Eph 5:5.

165. A rather less elaborate version of the *corona* or "crown" will be seen in the foreground of plate 19 in Lekai's *White Monks*. According to Peter the Venerable's testimony, the *corona* at Cluny was really quite splendid. In the *Statutes* he restricts its use somewhat, partly because it was a very expensive apparatus, partly because he felt that its impact was lessened if it was lit up too often (no. 52, PL 1039). The austerity in church furnishing inculcated by St Bernard was traditional in Cistercian churches from the time of Stephen Harding. Cf. *Ex. Magn.*, I, 21 (ed. Griesser, p. 28).

166. Père Anselme Dimier suggests that this refers to the candelabrum which stood at the sanctuary entrance in Saint-Remy at Rheims (*L'art Cistercien*, p. 35).

167. Cf. Eccles 1:2.

eyes of the rich, and amusement is provided for the curious, while the needy have not even the necessities of life.

What sort of respect is shown for the saints by placing their images on the floor to be trampled underfoot? People spit on the angels, and the saints' faces are pummelled by the feet of passers-by. Even though its sacred character counts for little, at least the painting itself should be spared. Why adorn what is so soon to be sullied? Why paint what is to be trodden on? What good are beautiful pictures when they are all discolored with dirt? Finally, what meaning do such things have for monks, who are supposed to be poor men and spiritual? It is, of course, possible to reply to the Poet's question in the words of the Prophet: "Lord, I have loved the beauty of your house, and the place where your glory dwells."[168] Very well, we may tolerate such things in the church itself, since they do harm only to greedy and shallow people, not to those who are simple and god-fearing.

29. What excuse can there be for these ridiculous monstrosities in the cloisters where the monks do their reading, extraordinary things at once beautiful and ugly? Here we find filthy monkeys and fierce lions, fearful centaurs, harpies, and striped tigers, soldiers at war, and hunters blowing their horns. Here is one head with many bodies, there is one body with many heads. Over there is a beast with a serpent for its tail, a fish with an animal's head, and a creature that is horse in front and goat behind, and a second beast with horns and the rear of a horse. All round there is such an amazing variety of shapes that one could easily prefer to take one's reading from the walls instead of from a book. One could spend the whole day gazing fascinated at these things, one by one, instead of meditating on the law of God. Good Lord, even if the foolishness of it all occasion no shame, at least one might balk at the expense.[169]

---

168. Ps 26:8.

169. Bernard's insistence that monks express the poverty and spirituality of their lives by the austerity of their buildings, is sometimes understood as a blanket condemnation of art. A closer look at this present chapter, however, reveals that Bernard's attitude to church art admits of degrees. He approves of whatever serves a devotional or instructional purpose, and considers bishops

30. There are plenty of other things that could be added, but I am prevented from going on by the burdens of my office, and by your imminent departure, dear brother Oger.[170] You will not agree to stay any longer, and you refuse to go without this latest little book. I shall do as you wish, and let you go, cutting short my words. In any case, a few words spoken in peace will do more good than many

---

bound to promote it. Secondly, he is dubious about the value of building grandly "for the glory of God," especially when it gives rise to scandal, cupidity or distraction among men. However he is prepared to cede ground here. Finally, he regards as completely inappropraite whatever has merely entertainment value. Grotesques are inexcusable in the cloisters because, apart from being an affront to the poor, they are inclined to distract the monks from their reading. Emile Mâle refers to this passage in support of his opinion that such images, whatever their original signification, were completely meaningless and devoid of any instructional intent by the twelfth century (Cf. *The Gothic Image, Religious Art in France in the 13th century* [London: Collins/Fontana, 1961], pp. 48ff., 60ff.; *Religious Art in France from the 12th to the 18th century* [New York: Noonday Press, 1959], p. 49). To understand Bernard's attitude it must be recalled first of all that he is speaking only of the decoration of monastic cloisters. For the medievals, who centered their lives and values rather profoundly on the sensorium, environment probably had an even greater impact on their moods than it does for us. To sit down to serious reading amid such a riot of amusing images was unthinkable. Bernard's contention that some people would spend the whole day fascinated by the grotesques may very well be less an exaggeration than we would expect. His attitude is echoed by Aelred of Rievaulx. "So in the monastic cloisters we see cranes and hares, deers, stags, magpies and crows. These are not the means recommended by Anthony and Macarius. They are more like the amusements of women. Such things do not accord with monastic poverty; they serve only to entertain the eyes of the frivolous. One who prefers the poverty of Christ to such pleasures of sight does not go beyond the limits of necessity. He would rather build shelters for his poor brothers than construct buildings of such extravagant proportions and unnecessary height. Enter such a one's church and you will find no paintings, no statues, no carpets spread over marble floors. The walls will not be covered with murals depicting pagan legends or royal battles or even scenes from Scripture. There will be no wonderful blaze of candle-light reflected on shining vessels. . . ." (*Speculum Caritatis*, II, 24; PL 195: 572cd; trans. Walker and Webb, *The Mirror of Charity* (London: Mowbrays, 1962), pp. 74f.).

170. Cf. Introduction, p. 8. Oger was a canon regular of Mont-Saint-Eloi at the time the Apologia was composed. In 1125 he became superior of a new foundation at St Médard in Tournai, and was abbot of this house for fourteen years. His resignation from office provoked Bernard's *Letter* 87 (trans. James, no. 90).

which give rise to scandal. I do hope that these few things I have written will not cause scandal, even though I realize that my condemnation of vices must offend those concerned. Yet, if God so will, it could happen that those whom I fear to vex will be grateful for what I say, and will give up their vices. I mean that the more austere monks will stop belittling others, and that those who have been remiss in the past will put an end to their excesses.[171] In this way both sides can maintain their own values, but without passing judgment on those who think differently. A good man should not be envious of those who are better, and the man who thinks his own course of action good, should not despise a lesser good that another has. The monk who can live austerely should not be harsh toward those who cannot, but at the same time he should avoid modeling his conduct on theirs. Those who cannot live austerely should admire those who can, but they shouldn't imitate them injudiciously. For, just as there is danger of apostasy if a man render less than he vowed, so too, there is danger that those who try to do too much will come to grief.

On Monks who come to us from other Observances and afterwards leave[172]

31. Some monks I have known, who have come to us from other communities and observances, who have knocked and gained admittance, have scandalized their brothers by their thoughtless departure, and have been no advantage to us, upsetting us by their wretched conduct. They scorned what they had, and foolishly coveted what was beyond them. However, by the due outcome of it all, God has made known how worthless they were. Fecklessly they let go of what recklessly they had snatched at, and they

171. That such a statement is included in a hastily written conclusion may indicate that Bernard himself regarded the two parts of the *Apologia* as constituting a single unit, that he is just as serious in his rebuke to detractors as he is in denouncing the abuses of Cluny. Cf. Introduction, p. 27.

172. This problem is treated more amply in *Monastic Obligations and Abbatial Authority, infra*, p. 138ff, no. 45ff.

returned discredited to the place they had left with so little fore-thought. The fact is that they had sought our cloisters more because they were dissatisfied with your Order, than from any desire of ours. What sort of monks they were was revealed by their flitting back and forth, from you to us, and from us to you, a scandal to us and to you and to every decent man. I have known monks who, under God's inspiration, have begun bravely, and with his help have bravely persevered. Nevertheless it is always safer to carry on with a good work already begun, than to begin afresh on something we might never finish.[173] I pray that we may all try to do this, in order that, as the Apostle says, "all that we do may be done in love."[174]

This is what I think about your Order and ours. This is the sort of thing I say to our monks, and this is what I say, not about you but to you, as you yourself, and anyone who knows me as you do can best testify. Whatever is praiseworthy in your monks I praise and extol.[175] On the other hand, to you and to my other friends I point out whatever is worthy of reproach, in order that it may be corrected. This is not slander, but candor, and I ask you very earnestly, always to do the same for us. Goodbye.

---

173. This characteristic affirmation of principle has numerous parallels: *Monastic Obligations and Abbatial Authority*, no. 46 (*S. Bern. Op.* III, p. 285; *infra* p. 140); *Letter* 32, 3 (PL 138b; trans. James, no. 33, p. 67); *Letter* 78, 13 (PL 199c; trans. James, no. 80, p. 118); and the letter to a monk who wished to become a hermit published by Leclercq in *Etudes sur S. Bernard et le texte de ses écrits* (Rome: Analecta S.O.C., 1953), pp. 138ff. Cf. Guerric of Igny, Sermon 1, 3 on the feast of St Benedict (*Monastic Studies*, no. 3, p. 4).

174. 1 Cor 16:14.

175. Cf. *Letter* 78, 7: "I am all the more bound to lift up my voice and praise the good when I see it for having boldly denounced former evils or else, were I to cry out against what is evil and say nothing about what is good, I would prove myself a mere backbiter and not a reformer, one who would rather carp at evil than remedy it" (PL 195c; trans. James, no. 80, p. 114).